W9-AZP-917

Standing and Delivering

What the Movie Didn't Tell

Henry Gradillas and Jerry Jesness

Foreword by Jaime Escalante

ROWMAN & LITTLEFIELD EDUCATION
A division of
ROWMAN & LITTLEFIELD PUBLISHERS, INC.
Lanham • New York • Toronto • Plymouth, UK

Published by Rowman & Littlefield Education
A division of Rowman & Littlefield Publishers, Inc.
A wholly owned subsidiary of The Rowman & Littlefield Publishing Group,
Inc.
4501 Forbes Boulevard, Suite 200, Lanham, Maryland 20706
http://www.rowmaneducation.com

Estover Road, Plymouth PL6 7PY, United Kingdom

British Library Cataloguing in Publication Information Available

Library of Congress Cataloging-in-Publication Data

Gradillas, Henry, 1934–
 Standing and delivering : what the movie didn't tell / Henry Gradillas and
Jerry Jesness.
 p. cm.
 ISBN 978-1-60709-942-0 (cloth : alk. paper) — ISBN 978-1-60709-943-7
(pbk. : alk. paper) — ISBN 978-1-60709-944-4 (electronic)
 1. Educational change—United States. 2. James A. Garfield High School
(Los Angeles, Calif.) 3. Stand and deliver. I. Jesness, Jerry. II. Title.

LA217.2.G725 2010
 371.2'07—dc22   2010025137

♾™ The paper used in this publication meets the minimum requirements of
American National Standard for Information Sciences—Permanence of Paper
for Printed Library Materials, ANSI/NISO Z39.48-1992.

Printed in the United States of America

Dedicated to Jaime Escalante

and the students and faculty

of Garfield High School

Contents

Foreword

If some colleagues called the eighties the decade of the dynasty of Garfield High School, they were not mistaken. To date, no school or school district has duplicated the success and the academic fame that Garfield High School enjoyed in that decade. Year after year the number of students that took and passed the Advanced Placement (AP) calculus exams grew progressively and impressively. As time passed, AP participation increased in other subjects as well, so the number of Garfield High School students participating in AP classes and taking AP examinations soon became larger than those of almost every other school in the country.

In the early 1970s Garfield High School was in danger of losing its accreditation. It was then that I met Henry Gradillas, at that time a Garfield science teacher. In 1975 all of the higher-level administrators were removed by order of the California Department of Education. Henry was appointed dean of boys, which made him part of what the Garfield faculty called the "accreditation team." I received a lot of help from Henry with the establishment of my math enrichment program. In 1977, Henry left us when he was promoted to assistant principal of a nearby middle school.

In 1980 I was behind the effort to collect signatures from parents and teachers of Garfield High School students for a petition to make Henry the principal there. The Los Angeles Unified School District (LAUSD) granted our petition and promoted Henry, who at the time was the principal of a small LAUSD alternative school, to principal of our school. Henry and I again began working together, as we continued to do for the next six years.

I felt confident about reaching success teaching at Garfield. Henry certainly understood the needs and obligations of an administration that desired to put Garfield High School on the map. In order to reach this goal, Henry gradually eliminated nonessential classes, or "Mickey Mouse" classes as I used to call them, in which students earned credits for studying subjects like consumer math, high school science, magic circles, student services, arts, and plastics. He replaced them with academic classes: algebra, physics, chemistry, and reading/writing, classes that he considered important for students to take in order to prepare themselves for college or a university.

Perhaps some readers of this book will conclude that my praise for Henry is exaggerated or extreme. It is not. Henry Gradillas always backed and worked with me and with every other Garfield teacher who was truly dedicated to teaching, and he was always ready to assist the student who had the *ganas* to succeed. Gradillas also provided orientation to parents to help them understand their responsibilities. He laid the groundwork that enabled administrators, counselors, and teachers to work together in order to make Garfield High School a school with a future.

Today we behold the products of Garfield High School's dynasty: professionals of prestige in various fields, engineering, medicine, and education to name a few. Without Henry's participation as principal, Garfield High School would never have yielded the success that it did. Henry was the right person in the right job at the right time, and he truly deserves a lot of credit for what took place under his watch at Garfield High School in East Los Angeles.

Jaime Escalante,
Garfield High School calculus teacher

Preface

In 2000 I had the good fortune to interview Jaime Escalante, the inner-city calculus teacher whose students' phenomenal success with the Advanced Placement calculus exam made him the subject of the film *Stand and Deliver*. At the beginning of the interview, I asked Escalante the secret of his success. His first words were, "Our principal, Henry Gradillas, gave us one hundred percent."

As Gradillas freely admits, Escalante's calculus program was entirely Escalante's own. Escalante set it up, taught many of the classes, chose and helped train the teachers who taught other calculus classes and the feeder classes that led to calculus, established the East Los Angeles College summer program for Garfield students, and convinced private foundations to foot many of the bills. Nevertheless, as Escalante freely admits, Gradillas's leadership created an environment in which quality educational programs like Escalante's could flourish.

Statistics bear this out. Escalante's program peaked in 1987, Gradillas's last year at Garfield, with eighty-five students scoring 3 or higher on the AP calculus exam. Within three years of Gradillas's departure, Escalante would leave Garfield in frustration. A year later, Angel Villavicencio, the Escalante acolyte who took over Garfield's AP calculus classes, would follow him out the door. Three years after that, Garfield's AP calculus program had become a mere shadow of its former self. By 1996, the number of Garfield students who had scored 3 or higher on the AP calculus exam had dwindled to eleven.

Escalante's success was not the only star in Principal Gradillas's crown. When he began as principal, the average reading level of Garfield's entering sophomores was 5.2, equivalent to the reading level of an average student in the second month of fifth grade. Several semesters after Gradillas established a reading lab and required all students who read at least three grades below level to take additional remedial English and reading classes, scores improved dramatically. By 1986 the average Garfield senior read at a tenth-grade level. While this was still short of the national average, five years of progress in three years with a population that had made less than average progress in elementary and middle school is impressive.

Under his watch, algebra became a requirement for all Garfield students. The number of English as a second language (ESL) students was reduced by more than half after Garfield redesigned the ESL program to help students master English within two years. The number of vocational courses offered at Garfield dropped by more than half after non-state-of-the-art classes were eliminated, and the number of academic courses increased substantially. The number of sections of chemistry offered increased from only one in 1982 to sixteen in 1986. The dropout rate decreased from 51 percent to 19 percent.

During his tenure at Garfield, the number of AP tests taken increased from 56 to 357. While he was principal at Los Angeles's Birmingham High School, the number of advanced placement exams taken there increased from 256 to 550. While he was at Garfield, the number of students entering colleges and universities increased eightfold. While it was once rare for Garfield graduates to attend any college at all, by the mid-eighties several Garfield graduates had received acceptance and full scholarships from the Ivies, UC colleges, Cal Tech, MIT, and Stanford.

Nor was his impact limited to promoting high-level academic classes. Average math scores for Garfield seniors on the Comprehensive Test of Basic Skills soared from the nineteenth to the seventy-fourth percentile. He is credited with decreasing campus violence and creating an orderly environment at both Garfield and Birmingham. He established a number of programs to support the progress of both high-achieving and underachieving students. During his tenure at Garfield, the number of students attending summer school classes increased from 260 to over 2,150. In 1986 the Los Angeles Unified School District recognized Garfield High School as the school with the lowest number of expulsions, suspensions, and incidences of police intervention in the district.

There has been a lot of wailing and chest beating about the futility of bringing academic excellence to schools that serve low-income, ethnic-minority children. Even after years of legislation aimed at eliminating the achievement gap between ethnic and socioeconomic groups, we still see editorials declaring that test scores are more closely linked to bank accounts and zip codes than to schools.

It is true that a lot of reforms geared to leveling the playing field for all American schools have failed, but Gradillas's formula proved itself effective two decades ago. The Holy Grail that twenty-first-century educators seek was at Garfield High School in the eighties.

I found Gradillas's formula for effective schools to be a logical one: establish a positive school climate, promote quality instruction, establish a rigorous curriculum, support teachers, provide support programs for students, hold students responsible for their behavior and their academic progress, and enforce the rules. He believes strongly that the principal has both the authority and the responsibility to promote learning.

He compares the mission of principals with that of military officers. "Sometimes you have to sacrifice a few individuals to save the platoon," he said. If a few arrests and transfers to other schools are needed to make a school an orderly place where learning can occur, so be it. The dramatic plunge in dropout rates indicates that his management did save the Garfield platoon. I also found in him a serious intellectual streak, deep understanding of and caring for his students, and incredible skills in motivating people, both students and employees.

Unfortunately history has for the most part ignored Gradillas's lessons. Virtually all American educators have "learned" the lessons of *Stand and Deliver*. They need to learn lessons of the real Garfield High. The Hollywood docudrama is extremely popular with the education establishment. Edward James Olmos claims, probably with accuracy, that *Stand and Deliver* was the most viewed film of its decade. Students of pedagogy view it in their education classes, teachers view it at inservice sessions, and secondary students view it in their math classes.

In the film, a star teacher single-handedly took a group of underachieving students from fractions to calculus in a single year. The reality was different. When Escalante started teaching at Garfield, the school was on the verge of losing its accreditation. Leadership was weak and order was lacking. After two hours on the job, Escalante went to the office, called Burroughs, his former employer, and asked for his old job back. He later changed his mind, in part because he found some basic math students who were willing to learn algebra, and in part because the state ordered that the old administration be replaced.

When I asked Escalante about the accuracy of the film, he said that much of what was depicted in the film was accurate, but added, "The kids didn't behave like the kids in the film. When Lou Diamond Phillips threw the chair . . . that wouldn't have happened. Mr. Gradillas wouldn't have allowed that."

After Gradillas's third year at Garfield, his success there was obvious to the LAUSD central office, or "Downtown," as it is known within the district. Escalante's program had become famous locally well before the film was made. When personnel from the central office asked Gradillas his formula for success, he spoke about requiring students to take academic classes alongside remedial classes, denying activities to students with poor academic skills, setting up supplementary classes at a nearby community college, recruiting teachers directly from college, calling the police in criminal matters, and transferring chronically misbehaving students to other campuses.

The district leadership was less than impressed. Rather than praising Gradillas and beginning the process of putting his management style in place in other LAUSD schools, the superintendent told him, "You can't do that." Clearly he could, he did, and his program worked, but the system was not interested. As Gradillas said, they wanted something that they could patent, a gimmick that could be set out in pamphlet format and taught to administrators in a two-day workshop.

Gradillas had been promised that upon completion of his doctorate he would be given a position as an upper-level district administrator. After serving six years as principal of Garfield, he took a one-year sabbatical to finish his doctorate at Brigham Young University. Upon his return he was offered a position not as an administrator who would influence academic matters, but as a supervisor of asbestos removal.

His career did not suffer. Bill Honig, superintendent of the California Department of Education, offered him a position of special assistant. Nevertheless, the end of the Garfield math dynasty was at hand. Within three years of Gradillas's departure, Escalante was gone as well. Within a few more years, many of Garfield's gains had evaporated.

FINDING GREAT MINDS TO LEAD AMERICA INTO A BRIGHT FUTURE

As the economy becomes ever more global and as Asia becomes ever stronger in the manufacturing and technology sectors, we hear the question, "Where will America get the scientists, the researchers, and the engineers to compete with the best minds of China, Japan, Korea, and India?" I saw the answer at a conference in Sacramento in April of 2005 where Jaime Escalante received the Highest Office: Citizen Award from the Center for Youth Citizenship.

There I met several of Escalante's former students, all former residents of the East Los Angeles barrio. One was an engineer who helped design the Mars rover. Another was working at JPL (Jet Propulsion Laboratory) designing fuel cells. Another was a program administrator designing and producing airplane components and tactical surveillance systems. A participant who had attended Wellesley on a full scholarship was the director of public relations for HSBC banks. Another participant, a former gang member who had suffered a knife wound in a gang fight while still in middle school, attended Harvard and became a dentist, a surgeon, and an exporter of medical supplies.

Where will we find great minds to lead America into a bright future? The answer is obvious: we will get the great minds that we need to keep America strong from the barrios, the ghettos, the rural areas, the suburbs . . . anywhere that there are effective schools to prepare them.

I was honored when Gradillas asked me to coauthor a book that will delineate and describe his techniques for effective school management. He is an administrator who has been on the front lines of education and has done what few other school leaders ever have done. Clearly he has much of value to share with both the present generation of educators and with all those who are interested in what is happening in our schools.

Although I share the byline, this is really Gradillas's book, and I am but the humble scribe. Except for Jaime Escalante's foreword, this preface, and the afterword, this book will be written entirely in Gradillas's voice.

Jerry Jesness, coauthor

Acknowledgments

First and foremost, we would like to thank Mr. Jaime Escalante, not only for building the exceptional math program that brought national attention to Garfield High School, but also for his dedication to his students and to education. May he rest in peace.

Dr. Wayne Bishop suggested that I write *Stand and Deliver Revisited*, an article that was originally published in *Reason* magazine. Dr. Bishop arranged my first interview with Mr. Escalante, who in turn put me in contact with Dr. Gradillas. Several years later, Mrs. Gayle Gradillas suggested that her husband and I coauthor this book. Without them this book would never have come into existence. Our thanks to them both.

We would also like to thank Escalante biographer and *Washington Post* columnist Jay Mathews for his assistance and for suggesting the title, and Mike Petrilli of the Thomas B. Fordham Institute for bringing our manuscript to the attention of Rowman & Littlefield's acquisition editor.

We also thank Rowman & Littlefield, acquisitions editor Rick Hess, my editor Tom Koerner, his assistant Lindsey Schauer, and production editor Melissa McNitt.

Chapter One

Who Is Responsible for Making Schools Effective?

I made a heck of a mistake at Garfield in 1983 when I brought in several area university professors to talk to our teachers. That was a mess because the professors and university administrators blamed—guess who?—the high school teachers for the problems they were having with entering freshmen. "The kids don't come to us prepared. They don't know how to read. They can't think. They haven't got any study skills." They pointed the finger at the high school teachers, and our faculty struck back.

A week later we had a faculty meeting, and I told the teachers that they had been pretty hard on the professors. Then they said, "It isn't our fault. Look who we get. It's the junior high schools. The junior highs are sending us nothing. The kids aren't prepared. They're chasing each other around the classroom. They can barely read. We don't have time to teach them enough to give the universities the caliber of student they want. What do you expect?"

Word of that meeting found its way to Griffith Junior High School, a Garfield feeder located about a quarter of a mile away from us. I attended a faculty meeting there where I got an earful. "I hear the Garfield teachers are bashing us, saying that we're sending them unprepared kids. It isn't our fault. Blame the elementary schools. When the kids come to us, they're lost. They don't even know how to walk in a straight line. What can we do in three years?"

There are a dozen elementary schools that educate the students that eventually feed into Garfield. I made it a point to attend a few of their faculty meetings. At one such meeting, I told the staff, "You know, you've been blamed for the poor quality of students coming into the junior highs." Guess what they said? "It's the preschools. The teachers there aren't even credentialed. Anybody can teach in Head Start. Most of the other preschool programs aren't any better. Look who we get as kindergarten kids."

I went down to some of the preschools. There are a lot of them around East LA. I talked to the teachers of three- and four-year-olds and told them that they were getting a bashing, that the elementary teachers were saying that problems in elementary schools were all the preschools' fault. They said, "Don't blame us. It's the parents. They don't read to the kids. They don't even talk to them. What can we do when the parents are sick or away working all the time?"

At a PTA meeting in East LA, I talked to about five hundred mothers, and I told them what everyone from the university professors to the preschool teachers had told me, that the educators at all levels say that it's their fault that their kids are unable to succeed in college. They said, "Don't blame me. It's my husband's fault, wherever he is. There's no parental involvement from him, there's no guidance. He abandoned us. What do you expect a mother to do?"

I found a bunch of men socializing and drinking beer at an East LA gathering, and I told them, "Hey guys, you're *culpables* (guilty). Your old ladies say that you're at fault. You're the reason your kids aren't making it in school." Do you know what they said? "Don't blame us. It's the culture, the history. It's Mexico."

The blame game also gets played in administration. A few years ago I was talking to a group of educators in Mobile, Alabama, and they told me that they have a problem there because they have so many African-American students. I have heard race and culture blamed elsewhere as well. In Oklahoma it's Indians. In Seattle it's Eskimos and recent Asian immigrants. In Yakima it's the migrant workers.

A group of teachers in Texas told me, "We envy Escalante. He told us he had the green light. You gave him everything he wanted: books, support, even a huge classroom. We can't do that because we haven't gotten the green light from our administrators. Escalante's situation was unique. Our principals have us in a stranglehold."

When I addressed a conference of about five hundred Texas secondary principals at Texas A&M, one of my questions to them was, "Why don't you give your teachers a little more leeway, a little more tether so that they can do some of the things that Escalante did?" The number one answer was, "The superintendent won't let us. We've got guidelines. We're bound by the curriculum. You were fortunate, Gradillas. Your superintendent didn't bother you." That was definitely not true. (There will be more about my relationship with the central administration in chapter 14.)

When I was addressing a small group of superintendents from the San Antonio area, I asked why they did not give their principals a little more wiggle room. Their replies were predictable. "We'd love to, but we can't.

We're bound by board action. The board has certain policies, and we have to follow them. We couldn't possibly make algebra mandatory for graduation. It's not in the book." I looked in the book. Nothing in the book prohibited it. It did not say algebra was mandatory, but it did not say it could not be either.

I met a board member that same day and told him what the superintendents told me. He said, "I can't do what you're asking. The state legislature won't allow board members to grant schools that kind of freedom." Later at a press meeting I met a Texas state senator. I told him that I felt that the state legislature had a problem, that the system did not allow freedom to filter down so that kids could get the benefit of teachers taking risks and doing things like Escalante did. His answer was beautiful. "We must be responsive to the electorate." In other words, it is ultimately the people's fault. If the people do not bring up the initiative, or the people do not vote, there is nothing that the legislature can do.

If you blame, blame, blame, what good does it do? Everybody gets mad, and nothing gets done. If you want to get anything done, you have got to do it yourself, at your level. Everyone involved in education, from parents to legislators, needs to say, "The buck stops here. I am a parent, a teacher, a counselor, an administrator, a businessperson in the community the school serves, a policymaker. . . . This is my job."

Chapter Two

The Power of High Expectations

When I visit schools, and I have visited schools in most of the fifty U.S. states, as well as some in Canada, Latin America, and Europe, the biggest weakness that I find is that students are not being challenged enough. Generally speaking, school systems across this country do not push students to perform at the level that they should. The reasons are varied, and most are not valid.

At Garfield High School in 1981 we had a population that was 98 percent Hispanic. Nearly half of the kids coming in there were labeled "limited English proficient." There used to be thirteen hundred students in ESL there. Many of the *vatos locos* and even some of the kids of the well-established families born in East LA did not know English well. They did not know Spanish that well either. That school appeared to have little direction, especially in the academic arena, because too many people accepted the conventional wisdom that serious academic study, or even acceptable school behavior, was beyond the students' abilities.

One math teacher, Jaime Escalante, was crying for help. When I began working at Garfield as principal, he told me, "I've got eighteen kids I've been working with for two years, and I want them to take this exam in calculus. Can you help me?" That was pretty tough. Out of 3,300 kids, we only had about three hundred taking any math from algebra on up. That made for a pretty small pool from which to build a calculus elite. Over 90 percent of our kids either were not taking math or were taking basic math, consumer math, intro to math, vocational math, and so on. Escalante used to joke that we even offered a class called fractions without denominators.

This was sick. We actually had more kids in gangs than in higher math, including algebra. In a school with over 3,300 kids, we only had one chemistry class. Imagine a school that large where we could only find twenty-eight kids to take chemistry in any given year. We had twelve kids in physics class. Sometimes Garfield only offered physics every other year. It was ridiculous. We did not offer a challenging curriculum to the students because of who they were.

I have visited schools that are 50 percent minority that did offer challenging courses, but the minority kids were not taking them. Consequently, the bottom line was the same. Both kinds of schools were failing to adequately serve all of their students.

There is a scene in *Stand and Deliver* where Escalante tells his kids, "You don't get it. We'll have to stay until six o'clock." One young lady gets up and walks out of class. Escalante says, "Heavy date?" and then comments that some of the girls need to be doing more work from the neck up. As she leaves, she tells Escalante, "I don't appreciate you using my personal life to entertain the class." He follows her out of the room and confronts her in the hallway.

What follows is a typical scene that I have witnessed countless times in many high schools. The young lady was in tears. She said to Escalante, "I don't know what's happening. My whole life's a mess. My mother doesn't understand me. My boyfriend's freaking out. Look at my clothes. I don't even have time to comb my hair. All I do is study."

Big deal. What you see here is a girl who is taking calculus because she is qualified to take it, because the last course she took and passed was trigonometry or precalculus, not consumer math. This young lady was so stressed out that she had lost her relationship with her mother, with her boyfriend, even with the rest of the world. Hey, welcome to America. Welcome to the real world. I have found that when kids are seriously challenged for the first time they go bonkers.

She saw that the rest of the school was not being challenged. Ninety percent of the kids at Garfield were either taking dingbat math, or else they were not taking any math at all. Why should she stay at school until 6:00 on a Friday? The girl was wimping out.

The problem was not that Escalante was stressing the young lady. The problem was that, as bright and capable as she was, nobody had ever put that kind of serious academic pressure on her before. She should have been stressed back in middle school, or even elementary school. Someone with that kind of talent should have been pushed years ago. Kids should not have to wait for their last year of high school to learn to deal with pressure and stress.

It looked like Escalante was losing her. He did lose some, but this episode had a happy ending. Because of Escalante's insistence, she hung in to the end, took the test, and passed. I ran into her a few years ago at a class reunion. She became a teacher and married another former Escalante student who is now an engineer. I asked her if it was worth all of the trouble. She just smiled and said, "What do you think?"

There is another scene in the film with a pudgy kid who slammed his fist on the board and shouted, "I can't do calculus! I'm the dumbest kid in this class! If I take the exam, I'll let the rest of the class down. I'm not going to take the test!" When one of the girls snickers, the boy shouts, "Don't laugh!" Then Escalante turns to the kid and says, "How can we laugh? You're breaking our hearts." Again, big deal. I know that kid. He took the exam, passed it, went to college, and now he is a civil engineer. A *cholo vato* from East LA with an average IQ is now a professional, providing a valuable service, earning a good living, paying taxes, and proudly representing his alma mater and his community. He was not a genius, but he was a kid who had an opportunity, who was able to say *"Con ganas lo puedo hacer,"* and who had a teacher who believed in him and was willing to push him. This is the power of education and the power of high expectations.

I've seen scenes like this over and over when kids are challenged. Image how many kids wanted out of algebra and geometry the first few years they were required in Garfield. The same happened in other schools where I have worked. Do you know why most of these kids want out of challenging classes? It is not because they cannot do the work. It is rather because they are not willing to pay the price. And what is the price? The price is time, energy, and effort. A lot of kids want to party Friday and Saturday. They want to relax. With minority kids you find this even more so, in part because too few understand what the ultimate rewards for serious academic effort can be.

I have found that, when kids are challenged for the first time, they will cry. They will jump up and down. They will want out of challenging classes, or they will want the teachers to dumb those classes down. If the kids happen to be minority, they bring more into the picture—racism, discrimination. "After all, I'm poor. My mother works as a maid. You can't be challenging me this way."

If kids are to succeed, they have to make a serious effort, and a lot of kids do not understand that. We are the grownups, and we have to get that message across. The kids who were depicted in the film stayed the course because of Escalante's insistence. It really makes a difference when caring educators push kids to do things that they might not be willing to do on their own.

At Garfield we did everything we could to keep kids in challenging classes. We told them that, if they dropped their classes, they were dead. We told them that the only way out of the tough classes was in a pine box, but we offered support. We provided after-school classes, Saturday classes, and summer classes. We got rid of classes that were not academic and began to provide remedial classes that were taken alongside, not instead of, academic classes. We had kids taking Algebra I, and then backed that class up with remedial math.

Eventually our kids saw the light. We had kids who refused to cover their algebra books. We figured out why. They were proud and they wanted everybody, especially kids from other high schools, to see what they were taking. They were proud that someone took a chance on them.

CHANGING ATTITUDES

In Garfield in 1980, kids who succeeded at academics were called kissies, suckups, *lambes* (boot lickers), and nerds. That is what typical Garfield students called kids who began to study. Imagine how Escalante's kids were ostracized. "You don't belong to us," they heard from some of the other kids. "You're traitors because you're taking a white man's course." Since when is math a white man's course? It is true that Anglos have used math to achieve, but modern math has roots in all of the inhabited continents of the world, in all of the races. Why shouldn't Hispanics use the same tools? I went crazy.

I brought the kids together and explained to them in groups. As Escalante pointed out, the Mayans were master mathematicians two millennia ago. It was the Mayans who first devised the concept of zero. As Escalante said, "Math is in your blood." Kids began to think, "Hey, we've got roots." I asked the kids, "With these roots, why are so many of you preparing yourselves to take the lowest paid jobs? Why are so many rotting in jail?"

Anyone who believes that Latinos and Blacks are five hundred years behind the times because they are brain deficient should not be involved in education. Education is *numero uno*. That is what does it, and everybody has to push it. Teachers and parents have got to push kids to get the best education they can get. Kids who are not getting an adequate education need to fight for the right to get one.

GETTING OUT OF THE CELLAR

When I was a special consultant to the California commissioner of education we found an elementary school in East Los Angeles, Lorena Elementary, with about nine hundred students K–6. One hundred and thirty-six of them were in the sixth grade. When they were tested in 1989, they scored at the fourth percentile. We checked the scores for the previous ten years, and none of them had been much better. The fourth percentile for an entire school is animalistic. I wondered why this school scored so low. After all, there were schools in the San Fernando Valley and Marin County with average scores in the ninetieth percentile range.

I guess nobody really cared, because this had been going on for years. I asked the state examination coordinator why this school was so consistently low. He asked, "Where is it located?" I told him, "It's in East LA, on Whittier Boulevard." Then he said to me, "Aren't most of the kids who go there . . . ?" Then I interrupted him and said, "Yes, most of the kids who go there are Hispanic. More than one-third of them live in projects. Most are on AFDC, and most are limited English proficient." He looked at me and said, "There's your answer."

BEING MISLED BY THE FACTS

Notice what he was saying to me. He was saying that the abysmal math performance was related to socioeconomics: race, religion, poverty, discipline, broken homes, single parents, mothers not reading to the kids when they were babies, and so on. I asked other people in my office what they thought. I got twelve reasons to justify the poor test scores. Those reasons had been accepted for years. Everybody, from teachers to administrators to curriculum specialists to university professors, must have accepted them, because nobody had done anything to remedy the situation.

There is no doubt in my mind that everything these people quoted me was a fact. It is a fact that these kids were poor. It is a fact that 40 percent lived in public housing. It is a fact that most were on Aid to Families with Dependent Children (AFDC). There is no doubt about any of this. Anyone can check public records and substantiate these facts. The argument falls down when people make a direct link between these facts and student performance.

We cannot do anything about the twelve facts. What are we going to do about poverty, other than provide the kids with a quality education? We can give the families a turkey for Thanksgiving or a basket of gifts for Christmas, but that will not solve their problems in the long run. What are we going to do about the fact that the parents are split up? What are we going to do about parents whose level of education does not even approach eighth grade?

Only 2 percent of Garfield parents had college degrees, and most of them were only living in the area temporarily, usually staying with relatives while they looked for a job or another place to live. The same applied to the parents of the kids in Lorena Elementary School. Believe me, there is very little that anyone could do about any of these facts, but, since people believed them, the school was just babysitting, and the scores stayed around the fourth percentile.

I went to the school and visited one of the sixth-grade classes. In that class, they had twenty-six kids present out of twenty-nine. Those absences were for legitimate reasons. Sixth graders in East LA do not ditch school. There is nothing for young kids to do around the housing projects. When I greeted those kids, they were bright-eyed and bushy-tailed. They were clean and well dressed. They wore the same brands of sneakers that kids across the country wore. Except for their dark skin and hair, they looked like kids from any classroom anywhere in the United States. Nothing in their appearance indicated that they belonged at the bottom of the academic barrel.

THE REAL REASON

I put a simple problem on the board: $3^3 - 7$. Can you believe that not a single student in that sixth-grade class could answer it? Although the state-mandated curriculum specified that by sixth grade students should at least understand squares and cubes, no kid in that class had a clue. A tear came to my eye when one kid touched the exponent like it was a flyspeck and asked, "What's that?"

When I began to explain that the exponent meant $3 \times 3 \times 3$, I began to understand why the kids scored so low. I put a triangle on the board and asked the kids to figure the size of the angles. I asked some questions about ratio and proportions, and others about probability. No one knew that if a spinner has four colored sections of equal size, the probability of the spinner landing on any one of those colors is one in four.

After a brief explanation, I asked similar questions about spinners with different colors and configurations. The kids were beginning to understand, and they gave me some correct answers. The reason that they could not answer my questions was not that they had brown skin, or that they lived in the projects, or that they were poor. It was because nobody had ever asked them to learn the material.

We went on to talk about two spinners, each with four different colors. "What are the odds of one spinner falling on yellow and one on magenta?" The first answer was two out of four, or one half. By the end of the session, a kid came up with sixteen. During that entire class period, not a single student asked to go to the bathroom.

It is no wonder that, when kids who lack these math basics go into biology, so many fail to grasp genetics. Kids who can grasp basic math concepts as quickly as these sixth graders did should not have to be placed in life science when they get to high school. If they can understand ratio and proportion, they can understand Mendel's genetics in biology class.

That year, we made sure that the kids studied that which they were required by law to learn. I dropped in from time to time when I was in Los Angeles, and we had these students take weekly tests based on the standard curriculum which we sent from Sacramento. We set up Saturday classes for those who were struggling with the concepts.

When the sixth graders took the state math test that spring, they scored within five percentile points of the state average, and they were ecstatic. The principal called me in, and she was crying. The parents came in and said, "This is wonderful. It makes our kids feel so good." When the kids took the Comprehensive Test of Basic Skills at the end of the school year, they scored higher than any class had scored at that school in its history. Guess what the CTBS test asked? Ratio, proportion, probability, and so on.

Why had those teachers not been teaching the content that law required them to teach? I talked to them. They were good people. They were not racists. They loved the kids. They bought items for their classes and for the kids with their own money. When a student from Mexico died, the teachers contributed enough money to fly the body back to Mexico and pay for the entire funeral. So why were they not teaching the kids? It was because they held little or no expectations for the students. The teachers really felt that the kids were so hindered by who they were and where they came from that it would be cruel and unusual punishment to make demands on them.

In *Stand and Deliver* there is a scene in which a math teacher says, "Teach calculus to these kids, Mr. Escalante? That's the worst thing that you can do. If these kids fail, and they will, what little self-esteem they have will be crushed, and these kids don't bounce back." The teachers really believed that any demands made of these kids would be so great that they would be doomed to failure. Then what are we going to do? Keep them poor, and on the welfare rolls, and in our prisons?

When we first required everyone in Garfield to take algebra, 70 percent failed the first semester. That is enough to get any principal fired. Can you imagine what the parents said? Some of the teachers said, "I told you so." The main reason that our failure rate was so high was that so few people believed that our kids were up to the challenge. Too many of our kids thought algebra was too hard for them.

Too many parents agreed. Too many teachers and counselors accepted that the socioeconomic situation of these kids was so low that they could not handle higher math. It was attitudes, not socioeconomic status, that prevented these kids from succeeding. History proved that. Within two years, our algebra failure rate became lower than the failure rate had once been for dingbat math.

After student successes become obvious, a school reaches critical mass, with success breeding more success. Escalante said, "You don't push kids up. You pull them up." When kids see friends and relatives, or even other

kids from the same neighborhood and school, going to college on full scholarships, getting good jobs, and making good lives for themselves, they understand that the same is possible for them. When they see their peers succeed in
academic study, they see that academics belong to them, not just to people of
another race or culture.

This is especially true in high poverty areas. Angel Villavicencio, one of
Escalante's fellow calculus teachers who later went on to create a successful
calculus program in the Chino Hills School district, commented that his
Garfield kids worked harder than the kids he taught in the suburbs, in part
because they saw calculus and their other AP classes as their only ticket to a
life they would otherwise never know.

Educators need to take a chance on the students' self-esteem and push
kids as hard as possible toward excellence. I guarantee that the self-esteem of
the kids who were in that sixth-grade class rose higher than it ever had risen
before, as did the self-esteem of the students of Garfield High School.

Chapter Three

Fostering Effective Schools

Everybody wants to live the American dream. The surest route to that dream passes through an effective school. It should be clear that all students, whatever their race, color, or income, deserve the opportunity to attend one. The formula for effective schools may be compared to the recipe for a cake. There are many variations that a baker can make on a recipe and still produce a good cake, but there are some ingredients that must be included and some steps that must be followed.

A blue-ribbon chocolate cake made with lots of sugar is of no use to a diabetic diner. As do bakers, educators need to take into consideration the uniqueness of the students, their community, and their teachers. Addition, deletion, or substitution of certain ingredients can make cakes and educational programs better suited for the end consumer. The basic techniques for baking a cake still must be followed, or the cake will not come out right. There are main requirements. First and foremost, the baker must believe that the cake can be made. There are certain parameters like bake time and proportion of ingredients. There are procedures that must be followed: mixing, pouring into a pan, and baking.

There are certain ingredients that must be present in order for education to succeed in any environment. Teachers must believe in the students. Students must be present. There must be discipline. Students must be held accountable for their actions. The content taught must be of value. Certain instructional procedures must be followed. Teachers must convey content clearly, and the content must be made palatable to the students. There must be some sort of evaluation that indicates to all involved parties that the content is actually being learned. Both administrators and teachers must work with parents as well as students.

The school must serve special populations. As a baker varies a recipe to meet the different needs of different diners, educators must vary instruction to meet the needs of diverse students. The variables should determine how to best deliver instruction, but not provide reasons to water it down. What we know of our students should give us reasons to challenge or make demands on our students that will assure academic and social success.

There is, however, a limit to the amount of tinkering one can do with a recipe. If the baker omits an essential ingredient, or if the cake is under-cooked or burnt to a crisp, it is of no use to anybody. If an educational setting is missing any of the essentials, education there will suffer. In order to tinker appropriately, those in charge must understand the population they are serving, the population providing the services, and the services themselves.

This knowledge will give an administrator the opportunity to play with the mix in such a way as to assure a successful product. Far too many educators, however, use the knowledge they have of their students as reasons to not challenge or make the demands that would assure academic and social success. This is always to the students' detriment.

By 1980 Garfield High School had been in a coma for years because previous administrations had used the usual excuses to avoid changing the nature of the school: the kids were poor, they were culturally disadvantaged, they did not speak English at home, their parents had little education, and so on. It is true that Garfield was a school that served a population that was woefully underprepared for the rigors of high school. The average entering sophomore at Garfield read more than four years below grade level. Few students had any serious knowledge of geography and history. Few students even showed any interest in serious academic study. Attendance was poor, and the dropout rate was abysmal. Many students had gotten through middle school without even learning the value of punctuality and regular attendance.

Given the academic background of our students, we had two choices: we could continue to teach them at the low level they had become accustomed to, or we could push them to catch up with the students from more affluent schools. Everyone knew that we could never catch up to Beverly Hills High School or the schools in the San Fernando Valley. Wealth did give the students in those schools certain advantages. Many of our kids did not have a quiet place to study. Many of our parents could not help their kids with their homework. Still, I knew that we could get close. (In one area, advanced placement calculus, we left Beverly Hills High School and 99.99 percent of the other high schools in the nation far behind.)

In order to remedy Garfield's depressed condition, we had to look at our school climate, the delivery of instruction, and our curriculum. We had to create an orderly environment where quality education could take place. We had to get the gangs under control and create respect for the authority of the staff. We had to help students build the study and work skills that the world beyond the schoolhouse would demand of them.

We offered every equalizer that we could. For students without places to study, we had to make the school available before and after regular hours. For those who needed homework help, we had to offer as much tutoring as possible. We had to get content through to the kids as clearly as possible. If we were to get our kids to pass the exams, we had to give them the knowledge that the tests covered. If we were to prepare them for the world of work, we had to help provide them with the skills they needed to succeed in jobs that existed in our community. If we were to prepare them for college, we had to provide them with the knowledge and skills that universities asked of their entering freshmen. All of this was within our power, as it is within the power of any school. In this book, I hope to share the recipe for student success that we experienced at Garfield High School in the 1980s.

Chapter Four

Establishing a Positive School Climate

School climate is the number one issue. For schools that are not functioning well, school climate controls everything else. If the school climate is not right, quality instruction is impossible. If there is little order and respect, even the best staff cannot adequately deliver instruction. At the root of the school climate is the way the students feel about themselves and the way the staff, the students, their parents, the alumni, and the community feel about the school.

INDICATORS OF SCHOOL CLIMATE

There are several indicators of school climate that are immediately obvious to anyone who walks into a school. When kids are in class and not in the halls between classes, when the campus is clean, and staff and students are engaged, a school is on the right track. There are other indicators as well. If school climate is good, more kids are going to stick around, and this will be reflected in the daily attendance and student retention rates. While there will always be disciplinary actions, when school climate is positive, kids understand the rules, and suspensions and expulsions become less common. When the community thinks well of the school, parental and other community involvement increases.

We all agree that the conditions under which teachers teach and students learn must be conducive to success. In order for successful instruction to take place, students must be present on a regular basis throughout the year. Teachers must have the complete attention of the students. There must be respect for teaching and learning. School climate does not only apply to the classroom, but also to the entire school and community. The main focus in achieving a positive school climate conducive to maximum learning is to establish basic rules and regulations dealing with the way in which students and staff go about daily work.

THE POWER OF RULES

Society operates on rules. Too often school administrators are guided by the belief that certain kids need to be given numerous breaks. The same sort of thinking that leads some educators to believe that kids from low socioeconomic backgrounds cannot master the Pythagorean Theorem leads them to believe that these kids cannot be held to the same behavioral standards as kids from the middle class. One of the "facts" that have influenced the education of Hispanics is that their hot Latin blood is going to keep them from sitting quietly through their classes.

It is certain that rules must be reasonable, and that kids should get second and third chances after they have paid some sort of dues, but, if a school is to be successful, order must prevail. Kids understand the importance of rules. Most of them do not want fights in the halls, nor do they want graffiti on the desks and walls, nor chronic disruptions in their classrooms. They certainly do not want gangs to take over. We did not run Garfield like a boot camp, but we had to assure that we had the same order and respect for authority that has to exist in any well-functioning organization.

It was especially important to not cut deals with rule breakers. It is tempting to give a good kid a break and avoid giving a minor consequence for a minor violation. In some schools cowardly administrators turn a blind eye to the excesses of some particularly difficult students. To do either makes the entire system look ridiculous. If the student council president can avoid a detention for being tardy, if a *cholo loco* can get by with insulting a novice teacher, or if a gang member can get away with a violation of the penal code, the respect for rules that there must be in order to maintain a positive school climate will not exist.

THE PRINCIPAL'S RIGHT AND RESPONSIBILITY TO ESTABLISH AND MAINTAIN A POSITIVE SCHOOL CLIMATE

Principals need to understand that state, county, and district guidelines prohibit any activity or situation that interferes with the instructional process at schools and therefore interferes with student learning. Nothing should interfere with the instructional process or the overall graduation goal. These rules are very specific. That mandate gives the principal the authority to insure that instruction goes on uninterrupted and mandates that all efforts be made to insure graduation.

I have found that many principals either do not know the extent of the power granted to them by these regulations, or, if they do, they are unwilling or unable to use it. I have talked to principals who told me that they didn't know that they had that kind of power. They do indeed. That is why they are called site principals. On the campus, a principal has more power than the superintendent. The captain of a ship is in charge of that ship, even if an admiral is on board. A principal is in a similar situation. I have surveyed the laws of many states and found this to be the case in all of them. Of course, if a principal errs, there is legal recourse. Principals are not above the law, but they are in charge.

During my first year as principal at Garfield, former students or students from other schools would park across the street from Garfield and turn their radios up full blast. This obviously interfered with the instructional program in the classes near the cars. The principal, teachers, and school security discouraged kids from parking there. Sometimes they would leave when so requested, but sometimes they would not. When they failed to leave, I asked teachers to tell their students to yell, "Turn your radios off."

Before doing this, I notified the local police. Other staff members and I asked the police to take action. At first the police told us that they could not order cars to leave as long as they were legally parked in a public place. I had to show a police lieutenant in writing that any deliberate act that interfered with the educational process is a violation of the law. The police then told the offenders that they must leave or be arrested. That was the end of the problem.

Some past Garfield administrators had avoided using such tactics to discourage noise makers. This gave the offenders the idea that they could come and play music at will. After the police visit, this never happened again. The police now realized that the school administrator had the power to stop activities that interfered with the education process. Administrators need to understand that this is the law and the power is there. It should be a given that an orderly school is the right of all educators and students. Look at the security around political conventions. Nothing is allowed to interfere with the nomination process. Nothing should be allowed to interfere with the educational process either.

INVOLVING THE ENTIRE STAFF IN THE CREATION OF A POSITIVE SCHOOL CLIMATE

All employees must help with the effort. At Garfield we had five administrators and about two hundred and fifty other employees. All employees, including the cooks and the janitors, had to realize that their number one mission was to bring all students along and educate them so they would have the choices that we wanted for all of our graduates. If a cook saw a student take an extra taco, I expected the cook to let the student know that that was not allowed. If a custodian saw a student drop a wad of paper or carve up a book, I expected him to intervene. The teachers needed to understand that they did not only teach subject matter, but that they also taught standards, morality, and behavior.

We had meetings in which I called the entire staff together. I told them, "No matter what your position is and what job you do, if I catch you turning your back on a situation, or allowing kids to fight, or refusing to discipline or report an incident when appropriate, you're not going to work for this school." Thirty-four hundred is a lot of kids, but 3,400 divided by 255 is not.

DEALING WITH DRUGS, VIOLENCE, AND OTHER VIOLATIONS OF THE PENAL CODE

Two things we would not tolerate at Garfield were drugs and violence. If students violated the penal code at Garfield, we turned them over to the police, and the situation became a matter for the courts. When those students returned from the courts, they were not welcome at Garfield. By the end of the first year, we were able to institute a no-fighting rule. Anyone who resorted to violence to resolve their problems was suspended, transferred, and gone the same day. This is not as draconian as it sounds. The transferred kids had the opportunity to make a fresh start at another LAUSD campus if they so chose. Some students continued their educations at a district alternative school.

Students who were at least eighteen could be placed in evening classes for adults. There were a number of other special programs available away from Garfield as well. The total number of transfers was not that high. Some pessimists told me that, due to the "hot Latin blood," fights were inevitable, and that I would end up transferring out half the student body. They were wrong. After a few transfers the kids got the idea.

ATTENDANCE

Everyone agrees that students must be present on a regular basis if they are to succeed in school. Teachers have told me over and over that it is hard to teach when they have a different group in attendance every day. Some teachers justifiably complained that in any five-day period, they would never have an identical group of kids. We had to take several steps to improve attendance. When students were habitually absent, all efforts were made to bring them back to school. After students missed two weeks, we talked to their parents to get their help to return their children to school. When students returned, they faced special difficulties. Returning to school after an extended absence is like jumping on a moving train.

Sometimes teachers would discourage students who chose to return after extended or frequent absences. Some would make comments like, "What are you doing back?" or "How long are you staying this time?" This kind of treatment discouraged kids even more. Even with encouragement from teachers, and even under the best of circumstances, reintegration was difficult. We came up with a special plan for students who missed two weeks or more. Exceptions were made for excused absences if the student had kept up with class work while absent or seemed willing to make a good faith effort to catch up on missed content.

Those who had been truant for two weeks or more from academic classes were placed in a tutorial room where they made up all missed work under a coordinator. Computer-assisted make-up work was available. This allowed students to return to class after having caught up. As a result, reintegration was more positive for both the students and their teachers.

At first some teachers complained about having to prepare make-up lessons, but they soon found the situation to be beneficial. Teachers soon discovered that it was better to let kids catch up than to struggle with them in class. The kids felt better about themselves because they had a better grasp of the material and they had a sense of having paid their dues. The teachers felt better because the students had caught up and done something to earn their way back into class. Students who were handled in this way were much less likely to repeat long-term truancy.

The AFDC program requires that school-aged children be enrolled and actively attending school in order for the family to receive welfare benefits. At one time Garfield clerks rubber-stamped approval for all student who were on our rolls, whether they were attending regularly or not. I instituted a policy of requiring an administrator to give approval only after checking the attendance figures.

The mother of one Garfield student came to me distraught after losing her benefits. "You are taking the bread out of my children's mouths," she told me. "No," I said, "You are the one taking the bread out of your children's mouths by not sending your son to school." After that, her son began to attend regularly, and within two weeks her AFDC benefits had been restored.

Continued long-term truancy on the part of students was first handled by parent conferences that resulted in a contract that stipulated that the student would attend regularly in the future. If the terms of the contract were not met, the student would not be allowed to remain at Garfield. One option was to be transferred to another school on what we called an "opportunity transfer." We would explain that, since the student obviously was not happy at Garfield, he would be given an opportunity to attend another district school. Actually, we rarely used this option for truants, although we threatened to use it numerous times.

The opportunity transfers were tit-for-tat with the administrators of the other schools. When we sent another campus one of our students, that campus would soon reciprocate, and we did not want to swap a truant for a gang member or a more troublesome student. We more frequently sent our truants to alternative schools, adult schools, and work-study programs that mixed academic study in the morning with work in the afternoon. As with students involved in fights, it only took a handful of transfers for students to get the idea.

PUNCTUALITY

Students reporting late to school, especially those coming in tardy to their first period classes, represented a huge problem. At one time, as many as 10 percent of Garfield kids reported late to school each day. This kind of behavior seriously disrupted delivery of instruction. In the past, Garfield students had been required to go to the attendance office and get a tardy pass, or "cut card" as they were called, and present it to the teacher.

After a student received three cut cards, detention was assigned. Few students actually came to detention, and there was no penalty for failing to do so. Cut cards were also assigned for tardies during the school day. I found it inexcusable for kids to be late. When I started as principal at Garfield, many kids paid little attention to bells. At one time, the number of cut cards issued totaled over twenty thousand hours of missed time in a single year. The cut cards really meant nothing.

Tardiness had to be checked, so we changed tardy policy to one with some real teeth in it. At first students who came to school late were not allowed to interrupt instruction in the first period class. Teachers were told to lock their doors as soon as the first period began. Students who were not in their first period classes were instead sent to the auditorium where their names were taken down and they were lectured on punctuality. Students were held there for the entire period. They were held responsible for instruction and assignments missed. At first, we had about three hundred students detained daily.

A second appearance at the auditorium meant that the student was referred to a counselor. A third violation meant after-school or Saturday detention. If a student skipped detention there was a mandatory parent-student conference. If it was deemed necessary, a contract was drawn up between the parent, student, and counselor. The nature of the contract varied. Sometimes it included a provision exchanging the first-period class for an after-school class. This was enough for students who had trouble getting out of bed in the morning. Some contracts stipulated that, if the situation persisted, the student would be enrolled in one of many programs available to students who did not wish to follow our rules.

After sixty days that this policy was in force, first-period tardiness dropped so significantly that we were able to use the cafeteria rather than the auditorium as the detention area. After this time, repeaters were rare. Very few students made it to three first-period tardies, the number that resulted in a contract.

We did, of course, consider mitigating circumstances. Legitimate tardies were accepted. When weather conditions made it impossible for all students to arrive on time, we held the bells, and students with physical handicaps or leg injuries were allowed to leave class a few minutes before the bell. Once a school establishes punctuality, kids know. When the number of tardies dropped below fifty per day, I was able to soften the rules.

Eventually we stopped holding kids for the entire first period. Since only a few kids were coming in late every day, allowing them back into class within ten minutes of the start of class no longer represented the mass interruption of the educational process that it once had. When one tenth of our students were coming in late everyday, drastic measures were necessary. By the time that the tardies were down to a daily handful, teachers were asking that students be allowed to return to class ASAP, and I was glad to honor their request.

TARDY SWEEPS

We did not go to such extremes for those who reported late to classes other than first period, but we did not allow late reporting to go unnoticed. Teachers documented chronic tardies and counselors and administrators dealt with these problems. We also instituted tardy sweeps at different times during the school day. The kids had seven minutes to go from class to class. This was enough time to easily pass from one end of the campus to another. Still, many stopped to socialize with friends and otherwise kill time.

Some sweeps were announced, and some were unannounced. During a sweep, teachers were asked to lock their doors. Administrators, counselors, janitors, substitute teachers, and some regular teachers who had volunteered to give up the first few minutes of their conference periods, usually forty or fifty staff members, swept the area, both inside and outside the building. Members had specific areas to cover, so they knew their territory, including the good hiding places. Teachers were encouraged to stand by their doors. During the announced sweeps, teachers would count down in unison, "two minutes . . . one minute and forty-five seconds. . . ," and so on.

Kids caught in tardy sweeps were taken to the auditorium. Later, as the numbers dwindled, the cafeteria was used. We rounded up about two hundred kids in each of the first tardy roundups. After three months, the daily average number dropped to about ten. In many instances, those caught in tardy sweeps were non-Garfield students, either dropouts or students enrolled in other schools. In the latter case, we contacted counselors from the neighboring schools.

I did get some static about the tardy policies at first. Some teachers at first refused to lock out tardy students, and a few even hid hallway stragglers in their classrooms. One teacher told me, "These Latino kids have had enough doors slammed in their faces. I don't want to slam my door on them." That teacher did not understand. We were not closing doors on their futures. We were rather helping to open them. We were teaching kids skills that they needed to make it in the post–high school world. Nineteen-year-old high school graduates should not lose jobs because they have not figured out that they have to show up for work on time.

COMPLIANCE WITH CLASSROOM RULES

If there is to be a school climate that is conducive to learning, teachers must be in charge of their classes. It will not do to have students refusing teacher directives or acting in a disrespectful manner in class. If all classes are to have a climate in which teachers can do the job that the taxpayers pay them to do, there must be consequences for not complying with teachers' rules.

Teachers are the first line in student intervention if the matter is not a serious disruption or a violation of the law. Minor matters such as occasionally not doing homework, chewing gum, or talking out of turn should be handled in the classroom. I asked my teachers to first confront students about these minor violations. If the behavior persisted, the teachers were to contact the parents. If that did not resolve the situation, the counselors were the second line of defense.

THE ROLE OF THE COUNSELORS

Of all of the groups I dealt with at Garfield, the counselors were the hardest to win over. An administrator who wants to improve a school really needs the support of the counseling department. After all, they control the master schedule. I wanted to change the role of the counselors from that of programmers to that of real counselors. A clerk can program and schedule. I needed my counselors to work with kids, to guide them, not just schedule them. All of our counselors were concerned with seeing that the kids got the required credits, but I wanted them to push kids to get the classes that they needed to maximize their potential.

Some counselors felt they knew and understood the kids better than other Garfield educators did. Counselors need to be on the kids' side, but that does not mean that they should regularly side with them against the teachers. Sometimes counselors see themselves as safety valves. To a certain extent this is good, but it can go too far. If there was a dispute between a teacher and a student, I did not have a problem with a counselor speaking as the student's advocate, as long as this advocacy did not result in a lowering of behavioral or academic expectations. However, being on the students' side does not mean being their buddy, but rather doing everything possible to help them get a quality education. Sometimes that means tough love.

Some of the teachers were great counselors. Escalante was more of a counselor than many of those whom we paid to be counselors. Unfortunately, some Garfield counselors were not willing to work with kids to solve problems. Some were quick to bounce problems either back to the teachers or up to the administration.

When I began to make changes at Garfield, the counselors were among the last to accept the new rules. Many were accustomed to telling the kids, "My door's always open. Come and see me any time." I ended that practice and allowed students to visit the counselor only with a pass from a teacher or with a prearranged appointment. A friendly, chatty visit to a counselor could no longer be used as an excuse to get out of class. This in no way prevented students from having worthwhile conferences with their counselors, but it did reduce unnecessary classroom disruptions caused by students dropping into class late.

When a teacher asked a counselor for help in getting a student to do homework, I expected the counselor to support the teacher. After all, academic matters like homework are the teachers' domain. Sometimes the counselor would draw up a contract specifying what was expected of the student and what consequences there would be for noncompliance. If the situation could not be resolved by the teacher or the counselor, the administration would take over. By the time the matter had been handled at the first two levels, a lot of groundwork had been laid and a lot of documentation was available. Usually students who got that far had problems beyond those in a single class, and the administrator would be dealing with the complaints of other teachers as well.

BACKING THE TEACHERS

Teacher support from the school administration, especially from the principal, is essential. Some kids are masters at playing adults against one another, and, if students get the idea that they can play counselors and administrators against their teachers, then the teachers' job becomes extremely difficult. I supported the teachers and expected the rest of the administrative staff to do the same. If I felt that teachers were not handling certain situations properly, we discussed the matter privately, not in front of the kids. Once the kids figured that the administration would consistently support the teachers, they would challenge the teachers less often. There will be more discussion on supporting teachers in chapter 8.

When kids understand the basic rules and they understand that the rules will be enforced consistently, they fall into line. Kids need to understand that someone is in charge, that there are consequences for breaking the rules, and that they are accountable for their own actions. For those who do not understand these key principles, there are consequences: after-school detention, Saturday school, and, if all else fails, transfer to another campus where they can attempt a fresh start. I did not limit the power to assign such consequences to administrators. Counselors had the power to assign these consequences as well.

A psychologist once chided me for employing what he called punitive measures, telling me, "The desire to learn must come from inside." I agree, but first students must understand rules. Escalante's kids understood why they were learning, but they didn't all reach the level of intrinsic motivation on their own. It took Escalante five years to build his calculus program up to the level of success shown in the movie. Kids are kids. Not all of them can understand the reasons that they should learn, but they can all understand that too many incomplete assignments can result in a Saturday detention.

It is unfortunate that we sometimes have to rely on negative consequences in high school. It would be nice if our students came to us with a love of learning and a mature sense of responsibility, but, if kids do not learn a work ethic in elementary or middle school, it is our duty to catch them up. The real world frowns on people who cannot show up for work on time or who will not follow a reasonable directive.

THE RESULTS OF AN IMPROVED SCHOOL CLIMATE

After we got our school climate under control, we still did not see an end to all of our problems. After all, no one can ever get school climate to 100 percent. There were still arrests during the sixth year, but there were far fewer, and even the attitude of those arrested had changed. When I began at Garfield, kids who were arrested for violating the penal code at school left the campus kicking, screaming, cursing, and threatening. Many times I heard, " F--- you, Gradillas. I'm going to get you for this. I'm going to burn down this f---ing school."

The last arrest I saw at Garfield came with an apology. Instead of cursing the police and me, the perpetrator, guilty of drug possession on campus, apologized for letting Garfield down. When things like that happen, it becomes pretty obvious that the school climate has improved by leaps and bounds.

Chapter Five

Delivery of Instruction

Again, a principal cannot focus on instruction until school climate is under control. If kids are walking the halls during class time, consistently coming to class late, and chronically disrupting class, quality instruction is impossible. It is not, however, necessary to get the school climate to 100 percent. In fact, school climate will never get to 100 percent, but at 60 percent it will become possible for teachers to deliver instruction, and at that point instruction should become the absolute top priority. That is when administrators need to concern themselves with how successful teachers are being at conveying course content, what goals have been set, and how the instructors will measure progress toward those goals.

Too many principals get school climate under control and then stop. A principal who can keep gang activity under control, get the attendance up, and keep kids from walking the halls between classes will win respect from the community and earn points from the central office, but a school with a good climate but poor instruction and a weak curriculum is just day care.

TREADING ON THE TEACHERS' TURF

When administrators get involved in instruction, they will strike some nerves. Unions and individual teachers are delighted to see administrators working to improve school climate. School climate depends heavily on the administration, the students, and their parents, but many teachers see classroom management and instruction as their private domain and see administrative input there as intrusive. When the administration works to create a climate in which teachers can work, good teachers are usually willing to work to provide quality instruction. Sometimes, however, some teachers will rebel when they see administrators treading on what they consider the teachers' exclusive turf.

Good school climate and quality instruction feed one another. Good school climate makes quality instruction possible, and quality instruction contributes to a positive school climate, but it is tough and unwise for an administrator to crack down on instruction from day one. It is a lot easier to get teachers to cooperate with administrators on what they consider their own turf when they see that administrators have been working for them. Until that point is reached, which should not take more than two or three semesters, administrators need to tread lightly on instructional ground.

The main point of instruction is to assure that kids get to a certain academic level. Administrators need to monitor instruction to assure that this will occur. This will take a lot of time at first. Once a principal knows who the strong teachers are, less active monitoring is necessary. Schools like Garfield was in 1980 present a special problem for those who seek to establish serious academic instruction.

Sir Isaac Newton's first law of motion teaches us that an object at rest tends to remain at rest. This is true in education as well as in physics. Some Garfield teachers in the early eighties were actually happy with low standards. One told me, "If I wanted to work as hard as you are asking me to, I'd go to the San Fernando Valley. I came to Garfield to take it easy." We did manage to get that teacher a transfer to another LAUSD school.

PROMOTING SERIOUS INSTRUCTION

The first rule of instruction is that instruction must be in place. While that should be a given, in some Garfield classes in 1980 almost no academic instruction of any kind was going on. In some other classes the students were doing activities that were more appropriate for middle or even elementary school than high school. We had a certain number of teachers who were happy to hand out worksheets and let their classes go on automatic pilot. In some classes, teachers regularly showed movies while the students slept, chatted, drew, or did work for other classes. In one basic math class, high school students spent days on end playing Monopoly, supposedly to teach them about money. In a few classes, there was not even the pretense of instruction. Sometimes I would walk into a classroom and see teachers reading the newspaper while the students chatted and played cards. I asked one such teacher to explain what was going on. He told me that the first part of the period was instruction, and the second part was free time. How could a school afford to give free time to kids who came to high school poorly prepared academically? Those kids needed every bit of instruction that we could give them.

Fortunately for the kids, good teachers like to teach, and, given a school climate that makes it possible to teach, they will do so to the best of their ability. Some need a little nudging and some direction, however, and those who prefer killing time to delivering instruction need to get out of teaching, or at least into another school. As time went by, Garfield gained a reputation as a place where teachers were expected to work hard, but administrative support for them was unsurpassed in the district. Teachers who wanted to work in an environment like ours sought us out, and those who did not found positions elsewhere in the district.

GRADILLAS'S INSTRUCTIONAL PRIORITIES

Gradillas's priorities are as follows:

1. Students must be evaluated, and the evaluation should indicate a valid academic benchmark.

   The academic benchmark must be both challenging and attainable. It may change from year to year. Once students begin to experience academic success, educators can raise the bar. Both the rigor of the benchmark and the grades indicate the level of success of both the students and their teachers. I required my teachers to turn in their final exams. My staff and I compared these exams with exams produced by other current Garfield teachers, with exams from past years, and, when possible, with exams from other high schools and even colleges.

2. Teachers must strive to reach as many students as possible.

   Teaching is not a one-way street. It is not enough to simply present the material. The material must be made comprehensible and interesting for as many students as possible. This is especially true in schools like Garfield where there often was a wide range of knowledge and skills in a given classroom.

3. Teachers have to employ a number of modalities.

   This relates to point 2. Different students learn in different ways. They have widely varying levels of abilities and diverse backgrounds. Students also have varying learning styles. A teacher might present material with a lecture, delve more deeply with a group discussion, later review with a film, and finally have students research the subject on their own.

4. Knowledge must relate to the students. Students need to know how the material relates to their lives, why it is important to them.

Teenagers have been on this earth for only a short time. To help students understand events of the past, a teacher should relate them to the present. Bear in mind, however, that, although it is easier for students to understand that which directly touches their lives, it is probably more important for them to understand that which does not. Making students understand how events half a world or half a century away from them affect their lives is one of education's greatest challenges.

5. The material taught must be relevant.

The lesson must have a purpose other than to kill time. Does the lesson fit into the curriculum? Does it foster or enhance knowledge and skills that will be important to the student?

6. Material presented must be state-of-the-art.

While much of the knowledge we pass to our students is timeless, much is dynamic. It will not do to have vocational students learning to rebuild carburetors, any more than it will do to have students learn about borders that vanished or changed a decade ago.

7. Students should gain insight, the ability to think and to question.

All knowledge has value, and this is not to disparage the learning of essential facts, but it is also important to be able to analyze, synthesize, and evaluate these facts.

8. There must be a coherent lesson plan.

Even experienced teachers need to plan their lessons in order for them to be the most effective that they can be. For the inexperienced teacher, an unplanned lesson will result in anarchy. The lesson must have an introduction, a presentation, individual or group practice, discussion or application, and a recap. Within these parameters, the teacher should have a lot of latitude. Every teacher has his or her own strengths and interests, and the style of teaching should reflect them.

PLANNING THE LESSONS

I was not one of those principals who demanded that teachers turn in lesson plans at the beginning of every week. To demand lesson plans on my desk every Monday would have angered some of my experienced teachers. Demanding mountains of paperwork to prove that teachers did all that I asked them to do would have violated the trust that I needed to have between the administration and my best teachers.

Still, I expected planning and I did demand evidence that planning was taking place. When I visited classrooms, if I could see from the quality of instruction that the lesson had been well planned, I did not ask for proof on paper. If, however, the lesson was clearly unplanned or poorly planned, I asked the teacher to show me lesson plans. If they were in place but not being followed, I asked why. If they did not exist, I required that that teacher turn in lesson plans to the department chair on a regular basis until instruction improved.

STAGES IN A TYPICAL LESSON

At the time I was principal at Garfield, UCLA professor Madeline Hunter's seven-step lesson plan was the preferred model for lesson plans at LAUSD. The following steps were included in Hunter's lesson plan. I did not insist that my teachers follow Hunter's model step by step, but I did insist that teachers provide a plan that was coherent.

Most lessons will include the following stages. While lessons that cover simpler concepts will be completed in a single day, some more complex lessons could take weeks, so not all of the following steps would necessarily occur in a single class period.

Introduction

The introduction is to preview and to get the kids excited about the concept to be taught. Some biology teachers could clearly present Mendel's theory of genetics with a lecture on Mendel's life, others with a demonstration. We had one teacher who would dress up as a monk, and that worked pretty well for him. One of our teachers demonstrated Archimedes' principle of displacement by dunking students into a tank. We had a social studies teacher who would introduce his lessons by wearing period costumes. When he started a unit on the Revolutionary War, he would dress up as a Minuteman. When he introduced the Civil War, he would alternately wear uniforms of Union and Confederate soldiers.

Field trips can be of great use to introduce a lesson. We had one social studies teacher who spent his Easter break taking kids on an extended field trip of historic spots in central California. This served as an introduction to many lessons. Powerful, attention-grabbing introductions like these can really turn kids on.

Presentation

Presentation should follow the introduction. The presentation can be a lecture, a demonstration, a field trip, a reading, video, a combination of many of these. Our dunking teacher would follow his dramatic intro by dropping marbles into cans and having students measure the change in volume.

Individual and/or Group Practice

Teachers should allow students the opportunity to practice what they have been learning. Here they can do for themselves what they had just observed, or answer questions, or get involved in large or small group discussions. This can involve hands-on work, written class work, or homework.

Recap

What was the goal of the lesson? Were the goals accomplished? Why did we do it? If the kids don't see the point of the lesson, the teacher might as well have not presented it. A good recap can help students piece together what they had been learning over the past several days.

Evaluation

This should tell both the teacher and the student if the material is really understood. Evaluation can be in the form of homework, projects, or quizzes and tests. Homework, while important, may not be the best gauge of content mastery, since homework is easy to copy. Depending on the nature of the material covered, projects may be the best or the worst way to evaluate. A student who produces a working electronic device might prove an under-standing of a scientific principle, but a student who brings dolls dressed in Southern finery has not necessarily proven an understanding of the Civil War.

Tests may or may not indicate mastery, depending on their difficulty. When teachers "review" by providing questions that closely parallel those of the test, the evaluation is of dubious value. This makes AP tests, which neither the teachers nor the students have seen in advance, the most valuable evaluation of all.

Homework

For some subjects, homework can be critical. This is especially true for students who come to us years behind in their academic skills. Still, home-work must have a purpose, and the teacher must understand the purpose before assigning it. Otherwise, it's just busywork. There are three good rea-sons to give homework:

1. To prepare students for a lesson to be covered in a day or so. Going back to the subject of genetics, students might read a chapter about genetics to preview what they are about to study, or they might do some background research, like a biography of Mendel, or a reading about prevailing theo-ries of life science before Mendel.

2. To reinforce concepts previously established. If, at the end of a lesson, a concept is fuzzy, homework can serve to clarify that concept, especially for those who are having difficulty with the class.
3. To review concepts after a lesson and/or to prepare for a test. Often it is useful to give final review homework in a format that resembles the upcoming test. This is not to say that review homework should be a copy of the upcoming test. That would make the test invalid. However, if the test is to be multiple choice, review homework in multiple choice format would be an appropriate test prep activity.

WORKING WITH THE TEACHERS TO MAXIMIZE INSTRUCTION

Of course, when all is said and done, it is the teachers who deliver instruction, and the quality of that instruction depends most heavily on them. All of the administrative policies, curriculum guides, and instructional models cannot take the place of good teachers. Administrators cannot be in all the classrooms all of the time. Even if they could, no administrator has the expertise to make instructional decisions for every subject offered in a high school, so it is essential to have the right people in the classrooms and to support and guide them in every way possible. There will be more on this topic in chapter 10.

Chapter Six

The Power of the Curriculum

Once school climate is adequate and instruction is being delivered well, it will be time to concentrate on curriculum. It does not much matter if the lesson is well delivered if the lesson itself is of no value to the student. Of all that a school can offer, curriculum has the greatest effect on the trajectory of a student's life. It is hard to get into a good college without first taking college prep classes. There are open enrollment colleges, but those who enroll without adequate preparation often fare poorly there. Students who are exposed to the most challenging secondary school classes are those who have the greatest opportunities in both higher education and life.

I have personally experienced the power of curriculum. When I was a student at Roosevelt High School in East Los Angeles, I was, like most low-income East LA Hispanics at that time, tracked into vocational classes and dingbat academics. I did some painting and construction work while in high school, and that put me in contact with another world, one much more opulent than my own.

My first real venture out of the barrio was when I did some painting for my tenth-grade life science teacher. I was astonished at the material quality of his life. His master bathroom was almost as big as my family's living room. I asked him why his family could live so much better than mine. "It's education," he told me. "I have a teaching certificate, and my wife holds a degree in accounting."

I was finishing one year of high school in a nonacademic track. I had straight As, but in classes like basic math and life science. A bright fifth grader could have handled those classes. I was determined to get into the college prep track. At first the counselors said no. I did not have any of the college prep prerequisites, and I was going into my junior year. My mother went to the office and pled my case, and my life science teacher and some

ROTC teachers interceded in my behalf. I was finally allowed to be one of the few Roosevelt students to study in the college prep track.

I had to attend summer classes in order to get even the bare minimum of courses required by the University of California (UC) system. I had to take biology alongside chemistry my junior year, since my life science course did not count anymore. Algebra, chemistry, and foreign language classes opened doors to UC Davis and changed my life.

When I began as principal of Garfield High School in 1981, the curriculum there was very weak, much like the curriculum of Roosevelt High had been when I attended there. Students there were required to take only one year of math and one year of science, but the math or science class was not specified. We had seven different low-level math courses: basic math, high school math, industrial math, consumer math, intro to math. I had one name for all of them: dingbat math. All of these courses stressed the basic computation that our students should have learned in elementary school. Some of these "different" math courses even used the same book.

Most or our students then met the science requirement with classes like life science, physical science, earth science, or, the Garfield favorite, modern science. Modern science was the king of the Mickey Mouse classes. There was not even any math involved. The teacher demonstrated the principle of gravity by dropping an orange on the floor, and lab work did not get any more sophisticated than the vinegar and baking soda experiments that a lot of kids do in third grade. Instead of observing single cell organisms through microscopes and logging and analyzing cellular activity, students studied microbiology by coloring pictures of bacteria. The level of instruction for modern science was appropriate for elementary school, not high school.

Few Garfield students met their science requirement with biology, chemistry, or physics, as did most students at North Hollywood High School or Beverly Hills High School. A Garfield student could take dingbat math and Mickey Mouse science to meet the requirements for graduation, and still know no more about math and science than do students in more affluent schools by the time they begin middle school.

Our English curriculum was not any better. Few of our kids knew the basics of English grammar that they should have learned in elementary and middle school. Although LAUSD had a recommended reading list, few Garfield kid were held to it. While kids in the San Fernando Valley were reading *The Scarlet Letter* and *Macbeth*, most of ours were reading simple stories from low-level readers or, worse, having them read to them. Even though writing is an essential English skill, most of our kids did very little of it.

When I began at Garfield, scores on the Comprehensive Test of Basic Skills were abysmal. In 1980–1981, the year before I began as principal at Garfield, our seniors scored in the eighteenth percentile in math. When I complained to my superiors about the situation, I was told, I suppose to comfort me, that thirteen inner city LAUSD schools had scores even lower than ours. Great. Garfield was at the top of the refuse heap and not really in it. Not all LAUSD schools scored so poorly. Seniors at the Anglo schools in the San Fernando Valley consistently scored in the eightieth to ninetieth percentile range.

It was not hard to see why our test scores were so poor. These tests covered material that our kids had not studied. When we looked at the CTBS we found many questions that involved algebra and geometry. Most of our kids had no idea how to solve a simple linear equation or how to find the supplement or the complement of an angle. Nobody had taught them that. We found questions that involved the formulae for the circumference and the area of a circle and questions that involved knowledge of the Pythagorean Theorem.

We found that many of our students had not learned even these basics in the basic math classes they had taken in junior high school, nor were they learning them in our dingbat math classes at Garfield. Moreover, most of our seniors had not taken any math class since tenth grade. If our kids were not even receiving adequate preparation for a basic skills test, imagine how poorly they were being prepped for the SAT.

Our tests in 1981 revealed that 60 percent of our students were so weak in English and reading that they required remedial reading and/or remedial English. In fact, the average reading level of our entering sophomores (Garfield was a three-year high school) was fifth grade, second month.

CHOOSING TO RAISE THE CURRICULAR BAR

My second year at Garfield we phased out modern science, the lowest of the dingbat science classes. That year, I pushed hard to get as many students in algebra as possible. In the 1984–1985 school year, we required all students to take two years of science and two years of math, including one year of algebra. Students who scored below the fiftieth percentile on the Comprehensive Test of Basic Skills were required to take a third year of math. By 1986 all students were required to take three years of math, including algebra and geometry.

We were the only school in California to require geometry at that time. I got some flack about these choices from the central office, the union, and the counselors. The law, however, was on my side, as were the rules of the schools in the wealthier sections of LAUSD. The law specified that a principal cannot allow a student to graduate without meeting the state and district minimum requirements. It did not specify that a principal could not require more. Several schools in the district required their students to meet a higher standard than the district-mandated minimum.

Students at University, Beverly Hills, North Hollywood, El Camino, and Taft high schools were held to much higher curricular standards than were those from Garfield and other inner city high schools. When I pointed this out to my superiors, I was told that the graduates of those schools needed certain classes to prepare for college. A district supervisor had the audacity to tell me that most of my kids would not be going to college. I had him there. It was true that most Garfield students did not go to college. How could they when they had not taken the classes that colleges demanded?

CONVINCING THE KIDS

There was an additional responsibility on the shoulders of schools like Garfield. In the San Fernando Valley, parents were pushing their kids towards higher education and helping them to prepare for it. This was not usually the case in Garfield. Few of our students' parents had university educations. In fact, those with even high school diplomas were in the minority. A lot of our kids associated classes like algebra and chemistry with Anglos and college, neither of which they personally identified with. Since the push toward academic excellence did not come from the parents and the community, or from the students themselves, it had to come from inside the school.

OPENING THE GATEWAY TO HIGHER MATH

In 1984 we first required all Garfield students to take algebra. That may not seem radical today, but in the eighties requiring everyone in an inner city school to take higher math was heresy. Algebra is an important gateway class. It is the key to understanding all higher math except to some extent geometry. It is also a gateway class in the sense that it opens the door to college.

A student with little knowledge of algebra will fare poorly on the SAT or ACT, and most universities require at least algebra as a prerequisite for admission. Even though not all graduates plan to go on to college, it would be a shame to deny any of them access to higher education because they lacked a single academic subject. If some of our grads who choose to work in a trade decide to switch careers later in life, they should have the tools to do so.

Even students who never set foot in a college classroom should still not be denied the opportunity to study higher math. Before algebra, all math is computational. Algebra introduces the concept of the variable. Dealing with variables encourages abstract thinking. It shows students a different way to view reality. Geometry is more than the study of shapes. At the heart of geometry lie the proofs. Geometry teaches logical thought, an important skill for everyone, in or out of college.

Lack of higher math was keeping our kids from succeeding in the sciences as well. In 1981–1982, we had only one section of chemistry. Of course, people had the usual excuses—the poverty, the culture, the hot Latin blood, and so on. There was one legitimate excuse: most of our kids lacked the math skills they needed to balance formulae. The algebra requirement remedied that situation. By 1985 we had seventeen sections of chemistry, two of them AP.

REMEDIAL MATH, GARFIELD STYLE

We really did have kids in Garfield in the early eighties who were in no way prepared to take algebra, and we had to offer classes that would prepare them, but we wanted to break the cycle of perpetual low-level classes that they had experienced throughout their school years. We decided that those who lacked basic math skills would take remedial math in place of an elective, in conjunction with, not instead of, algebra. Whether or not our kids were ready, they would take the same algebra class that mainstream middle class kids in suburban schools took. We made the new remedial math tougher than the old basic math classes had been. We wanted the classes to be prealgebra and pregeometry, not just computational math. If a kid did not know the times tables, we taught them, but we expected those kids to study such very basic math skills on their own time or at special after-school tutoring sessions. Our remedial math classes stressed factoring, ratio and proportion, simple equations and inequalities, and areas and volumes of various planes and solids. Some special education students took prealgebra with a book called *Algebra 1/2* instead of regular algebra or basic math. A number of these kids did well enough in this course that they were able to later take algebra and succeed there.

Many complained that algebra was too hard for our kids, and we were just setting them up for failure. By the end of the first semester of the first year of the algebra requirement, the failure rate was about 70 percent. The 30 percent who passed went on to take Algebra 1B, but those who failed Algebra 1A were required to repeat it during the second semester. The failure rate for the repeaters was 40 percent. Those who failed Algebra 1A the second time had five options. They could take the class yet again in night school, summer school, or in regular classes the following year, or they could seek a transfer to an alternative school or another regular LAUSD high school that did not include algebra in its graduation requirements.

New students coming into Garfield who did not have algebra credit were placed in an algebra class. This included entering sophomores, students who transferred from other schools, and students who had not passed algebra in previous years. I once got into a bit of trouble for saying that I would rather see a student fail in algebra than get an "A" in a remedial class. At any rate, the students proved to be up to the challenge. By the end of the second year, our failure rate for algebra was actually lower than it had once been for dingbat math.

Some of the failures were really success stories. Some of the kids really were so underprepared that it was impossible for them to make it through algebra the first time around. Still, by having to take algebra, whether or not they were ready, they got the message that these are skills that they could and should master. This also sent a signal to our feeder schools that they had better send kids to Garfield with stronger math skills than just a weak grasp of computational math.

Many of the kids who failed algebra failed their first semesters in the mid-fifties, which indicated that they were picking up something along the way, and then did quite well when they repeated the course the following semester.

STANDING FIRM

A big part of the secret of our success was holding firm to our requirements. Students who failed the first semester of Algebra I were not allowed to spend their second semester in physical education (PE) or a vocational class. They had to take Algebra I-A again the next semester. If they failed again, they had to take it again in the summer. Since California and LAUSD allowed students to graduate with only basic math, at first we allowed some of our students to use their basic math credits in order to graduate, but not until they had attempted algebra at least three times.

The biggest problems came from higher up. After I set up ten new sections of algebra, I got called in by the area superintendent who told me that teachers and counselors were complaining, that I was moving too fast, and the kids weren't ready. The counselors were a very hard sell. In the summer of 1983, the counselors had scheduled thirty-six sections of basic math for the following school year. I asked them to change one third of them to algebra. At first the head counselor offered me only two more sections.

Students with good or even adequate math scores on the CTBS had already been placed in algebra. The remaining students had math scores that were dismal. I stood firm on my demand for twelve more sections. The counselors had to resort to using reading scores to separate the basic math students from the algebra students. The students who were reading at or even near grade level were placed in algebra along with all the students who scored well in math.

The response from teachers was mixed. Some resisted because they honestly felt that the students were not prepared for algebra, but Escalante and some other like-minded teachers enthusiastically supported the change. When the smoke finally cleared, it was the kids who came to the rescue. After the failure rate dropped below what it had been in dingbat math, the change became permanent.

The CTBS scores soared as well. Our 12th grade math scores rose from the eighteenth percentile in 1980, to the twenty-sixth, to the thirty-fifth, to the fortieth, and eventually to the seventy-second in 1987. By my sixth year, there were only two classes of double-blocked math per semester. By that time, our students had come to understand that Algebra I is not that hard, and that it certainly was not beyond their grasp. It was not a "white" class anymore. It was a Garfield class.

We upgraded the curriculum in other areas as well. We weeded out basic science classes and replaced them with biology, chemistry, and physics, and we improved the content of the social studies and English classes.

REMEDIAL READING AND ENGLISH

As happened with math, we had a lot of kids who had been in a cycle of remedial and low-level English and reading classes throughout elementary and junior high school. A lot of them had never read an entire book or a poem that was any longer than a limerick or a nursery rhyme. One of the CTBS questions that most of our entering sophomores missed asked the number of lines in a sonnet. Of course they missed it. In their remedial reading and basic English classes in middle school they were reading from collections of low-level stories or even basal readers. These kids needed to get their reading and English skills up to speed, but they also needed to have exposure to Shakespeare, Dickens, Twain, Dickenson, Hemmingway, and other great writers, and they needed exposure to various literary genres.

We decided that any student who read at least three years below grade level would get remedial instruction in English, which concentrated on reading comprehension, basic grammar, and writing. Like remedial math, the remedial English class was in addition to, not instead of, their regular English class. We hired some teaching assistants and brought in volunteers to help teach our slow readers in small groups or one-to-one. That way we were able to build literacy skills and teach such writing basics as spelling, language mechanics, and sentence structure and still give kids exposure to literature and other language topics that most American kids studied.

In 1983 we were able to convert an injection-molding classroom into a huge reading lab. Language arts teachers could send students with weak reading skills to the lab at their convenience. By 1987 only two remedial English classes remained. The reading lab, however, continued in operation.

LANGUAGE ACROSS THE CURRICULUM

Since language and reading skills were so weak among our entering students, I asked all of my teachers, whatever subject they taught, to address these skills. I asked that all teachers, even PE teachers, present at least thirty vocabulary words per week. I allowed the teachers great latitude in evaluating mastery of that vocabulary, but I wanted it taught.

I also asked teachers to dedicate fifteen minutes of each class to some sort of reading activity when that was possible. We did not follow this lockstep. I did not insist that science teachers interrupt a lab activity, but I wanted the reading element to be included whenever it was practical. I would not recommend this requirement for all schools, but Garfield was a special case. Given that we had many bright kids entering our school reading more than four years below grade level, this emphasis on reading and language was necessary.

WORKING TO IMPROVE STANDARDS IN FEEDER SCHOOLS

Part of our problem with basic skills resulted from low standards in the middle schools that fed us. That did not mean that this situation was completely out of our control. Math was a special problem for us at Garfield. We were only a three-year school, and few ninth graders were studying algebra in middle school. Without extra classes, Garfield students could only take Algebra, Geometry, and Algebra II. Escalante remedied this situation by setting up summer classes at East Los Angeles College, but we also worked to bring more algebra classes to the middle schools.

Even the few kids who were receiving algebra in our feeder schools in the early 1980s were coming up short. We found that some of the middle-school algebra classes were so watered down that they were really only prealgebra. Middle-school counselors were even encouraging many of their algebra students to take algebra again when they got to high school. We encouraged tougher standards in those schools by announcing that any student who had a

C or higher in middle school algebra would be required to take geometry in tenth grade at Garfield.

We encouraged Garfield students with siblings in our feeder schools to ask their parents to pressure middle school administrators to raise standards, and we worked behind the scenes with administrators as well. Escalante and I were once at a PTA meeting at one of our feeder schools where I overheard a middle school administrator complain about pressure from parents to add more rigor to his school's math curriculum. "I smell Gradillas here," he said.

PROVIDING ESPECIALLY CHALLENGING COURSES

Every school has an obligation to offer especially challenging courses to students who have the *ganas* to take them. I will go further and say that no school has the right to deny kids the right to take a course for college credit in high school. In the seventies, Garfield had 3,300 students, but very few honors classes and no AP classes. That is sick. Even a tiny high school with only a few hundred students needs to offer at least one or two AP classes. All students should have the opportunity to take college-level classes in high school if they so choose.

It is, however, important to do more than put demanding classes in place. We educators need to motivate students to take them and succeed in them. At Garfield we had a number of what I call NFGT (non-functioning gifted and talented) students. They had IQs that qualified them for the gifted and talented program, but not the grade point averages. A lot of them were taking Mickey Mouse classes and were in no way living up to their potentials. A lot of these kids lacked both motivation and study skills.

We also had a lot of bright, hardworking kids who never were labeled gifted and talented (GT) because they lacked English skills in elementary school when monolingual English-speaking kids were being tested for GT. Others may have not had the IQ to qualify for GT, but they had the *ganas,* and they did well in higher-level classes. We decided to mix GT and non-GT students in the same classes. This was done in rural schools with small populations, so why not at Garfield? The California rule mandated that 51 percent of kids in GT classes be labeled gifted but others could be admitted at the discretion of the principal.

I asked teachers for a list of kids who could perform in honors classes. We established an academically enriched (AE) program that mixed these kids with kids already in the GT program. In order to placate GT teachers who complained about this arrangement, I promised that any non-GT student who fell below a B in a GT course could be removed with no questions asked.

GARFIELD'S MAGNET SCHOOL

LAUSD offered several high school principals the opportunity to establish magnet schools within their regular schools. These were schools that offered instruction in specialized areas and that were open to students from all parts of the district. These magnet programs were better funded than most, with smaller class sizes, better materials and equipment, their own counselors, and some of the district's best-qualified teachers. There were several magnet schools with a number of different areas of specialization spread throughout the district.

My first year at Garfield I was offered an opportunity to house a magnet school on our campus. I requested a computer science/math magnet, and my request was granted. We got the program started the second semester of my first year at Garfield. By the beginning of my second year we had about two hundred kids in the program, about a quarter of which came from Garfield's attendance zone.

This was a great opportunity to start pulling up the kids in the regular Garfield program. While the Garfield student body was more than 98 percent Hispanic, and those almost entirely Mexican-American and Mexican, the magnet school population was an ethnic mix also including Asians, African-Americans, and Anglos. Having them on campus was a good cultural experience for our regular students, many of whom rarely left East LA. All of the kids in the magnet program planned to go to college, so in that way they were positive role models for other Garfield students. We hoped that the presence of demanding classes and college-bound students would give our regular students a "taste of honey" that would encourage them to follow the same path.

There was some concern that we would end up with two schools that were worlds apart, a small, elite magnet school for two hundred kids and a large, less prestigious school for the other three thousand. These concerns faded within a few years as serious academic courses became a reality for students in the regular program as well.

ADVANCED PLACEMENT'S ROLE

Escalante did not much like the GT label. He felt that anyone with the *ganas* to take an advanced class should be allowed to do so. Once, a student from a GT math class asked Escalante for help with a trigonometry problem. When the student explained that he was gifted, Escalante said, "This problem's for boy scouts. I'm not going to waste time explaining it. I'll let one of my students who's not gifted explain it to you." AP was the perfect program for some of our bright kids whose talents had not been identified in tests. Any student with the *ganas* and the appropriate academic prerequisites could take AP classes.

The beauty of AP is that it puts a school's students up against the best students in the United States. It also brings people together. In regular classes, there are always complaints from students and their parents about teacher-made tests. Someone always finds them unfair, and there are always kids and parents who want to bargain for higher grades. The system sometimes makes students and teachers adversaries. With AP, parents, students, teachers, and administrators are all on the same side. Rather than being the "enemy" who is punishing the student with poor grades or tests that are too hard, the teacher is the coach working with the students to help them meet the goal of passing the AP exam. If there must be an "enemy," it is the Educational Testing Service.

When I came to Garfield as principal, there was already a small AP program in place. Escalante had his eighteen kids. We had a number of kids taking AP in Spanish, and there were a few in English and history. I established a few policies to encourage AP growth. Teachers who volunteered to teach an AP course for the first time were given an additional prep period in addition to their regular conference period. This allowed them to brush up on the material, visit other teachers, and even visit colleges. I also allowed teachers to start up an AP class with as few as ten students.

Escalante had to do some statistical sleight of hand when he started his first class, since his initial enrollment was below the minimum class size allowed by the district, but within a few years his classes had grown so large that I had to get him a special classroom that was large enough to seat all of his students. Eventually, AP calculus enrollment grew to over one hundred.

Some teachers were concerned that creaming classes to get students for higher-level courses would water down the curriculum of the regular classes. The opposite proved to be true. Teachers who taught higher-level courses found that they brought content from those courses to their regular courses. Teachers commented that they found it easier to teach regular classes at a higher level after they had taught AP.

I allowed AP teachers three years to make their programs successful. If, after that time, enrollment had not grown to twenty or so, or if passing rates were poor, I would consider giving the AP class to another teacher.

We did all that we could do to decrease the number of roadblocks to AP enrollment. Of course, we did not let kids who had only taken consumer math or algebra into AP Calculus, but, if a student who lacked a class in math analysis had done very well in trigonometry and the calculus teacher thought that he or she was ready, we waived the math analysis prerequisite. At one time only students with A averages were allowed in AP. We found a lot of bright, formerly mediocre students who had seen the light and were really ready for AP, even if their transcripts indicated that they were not, so we dropped that requirement. We dropped the requirement that parents give written permission before kids could enroll in AP classes. Sometime that little piece of paper kept potentially successful kids out. Once kids were enrolled, we did require both them and their parents to sign a contract promising that the student would complete all required work, and occasionally we did lose some students because someone would refuse to sign, but, by then, they were already inside, and dropping the class at that point involved a process of meeting with the teacher, a counselor, and perhaps an administrator.

When a student enrolled in an AP class, we demanded a serious commitment. The contract demanded that all AP students actually take the test. I got some flack about that from some of the teachers the first year. The teachers considered this choice to be their domain, and that the administration should have no say in this matter. The test makes AP what it is, and we would not allow kids to avoid it. Fundraisers helped to pay the costs.

In 1985 we started having rallies for our AP participants. AP tests were always taken in May, and we did all that we could to get everybody to focus on AP in the weeks before the test. Teachers were asked to avoid scheduling non-AP activities during that time if at all possible. A few days before the exams, we called the entire student body to the football field and had each AP teacher bring his or her students forward to be recognized. This not only helped psyche kids up for the test, but it also showed AP in a positive light and helped convince other students, especially the sophomores, to consider taking AP classes in future years. Kids got to see that the AP students were not nerds, suckies, and *lambes*, but that they were their cousins, neighbors, and friends.

AP success at Garfield was a great example of Escalante's model of pulling kids up. When barrio kids saw their cousins and neighbors graduating from high school with at least a semester's worth of college credit, and they saw them going to schools like MIT, Stanford, Yale, and USC on full scholarships, and they realized that those kids were a lot like they were, they wanted a piece of the action.

THE POWER OF THE CURRICULUM

Nothing changed Garfield more than the change of curriculum. Nothing involved the parents more. At first it was because the kids complained. When students did not get to take the elective classes they wanted, or they got knocked out of activities, they went to Momma and Poppa. My staff and I were seeing three to four hundred parents per month. It got to where our advisory council had to meet in the auditorium. After the parents came to see the fruits of Garfield's new curricular change, we got steadily less complaints and more support as time went by. Gang activity and drug use decreased and attendance improved as kids realized that challenging courses were leading them to the light at the end of the tunnel.

Chapter Seven

Special Instructional Programs

It is true that one size does not fit all. Some students have special needs or are in special situations that require specialized instruction. Initially at Garfield, way too many of our students were determined to be in those situations, and only a handful had access to the education that was offered to average students in more affluent schools. The majority of our kids had been tracked into or had chosen vocational classes.

Almost half of our students were in ESL, including hundreds of students who had been born and educated in the United States and for whom English was the dominant language. Many of our immigrant students were locked out of the mainstream because they were spending years more than was necessary to learn English. Vocational education, special education, and ESL had their places, in fact important places, in our curriculum, but they needed serious revision.

STATE OF THE ART VOCATIONAL EDUCATION

Not everybody will go to college. At Garfield we wanted to make that option available to as many students as possible, but we respected the trades and business skills as well. We did, however, want to make certain that all courses offered at Garfield led to success for our students. When students leave a high school with a diploma, they should be prepared to enter higher education or to take a job that pays at least twice the minimum wage, or at least have the skills that will enable the employee to reach that point within the first few months on the job. If a voc-ed graduate ends up doing little more than sweeping the shop floor, something is wrong. Unfortunately, too many schools see vocational education as a track for less able students and use voc-ed classes as holding pens. Sometimes what should be preparation for well-paying jobs becomes little more than a total waste of time.

GIVING EMPLOYERS WHAT THEY WANT

Preparation for the workplace is more than teaching job skills. I have found that the most important qualities sought by businesses are not specific vocational skills, but attitudes and ethics. One manager told me, "We can teach an employee to weld. We want you to teach the kids you send us punctuality and respect." Another said, "We can't hire your kids if their attendance is bad, if they come in late or leave early." Also high on employers' lists are honesty, trustworthiness, and loyalty to the company. As one might expect, employers also want schools to send them graduates with strong reading, writing, general communication, and math skills. Some of the most important job skills are those that we teach in all classes every day.

In high school, vocational education should not be career exploration. Middle school is the place for exploration. High school voc ed is the place for preparation. When designing voc-ed classes, we got input from the community. We asked the owners of small businesses and the managers of the local operations of Fortune 500 companies for suggestions. We wanted to create a profile of what corporate America wants. It can be reasonably argued that the liberal arts are worth studying even if they do not directly lead to employment, but vocational education is all about job training, and what is the point of training students for jobs that do not exist or will not be available locally?

Inevitably counselors will direct students who are perceived as having low skills into general voc-ed classes. Vocational teachers should design higher-level classes with prerequisites. This not only saves teachers from burn-out by providing some periods filled with highly motivated students, it also provides poorly motivated beginning students with good peer role models.

When I taught agriculture at Belvedere Junior High School, I created a second-year course in landscaping for those who wanted to go further with those skills. Our students in that class took second place in a city-wide contest of landscape design in 1967. Students who have had two or three years of demanding specialized training in a vocational field will be prepared for hard-to-fill jobs that require specialized skilled workers.

VOCATIONAL EDUCATION THAT IS EFFECTIVE

Vocational education needs to be effective. At Garfield we had a plastic injection molding class in which each semester the entire class produced a single project, a pink plastic pig. During the class, the kids spent most of their time walking around the shop and chatting with one another. Obviously this was not a wise use of time. If the kids had been really learning injection molding, we would have left the class in place. I did give the teacher a semester to improve the course. At the end of that semester, his classes again each produced a single plastic pig, this time a blue one. Since the kids were not actually learning any useful vocational skills, we shut down the class and turned the room into a reading lab.

We also cut our art department down from six teachers to three. In our most poorly taught art classes, the kids were learning neither academic nor vocational skills. Instead, they were making simple sketches and doing activities like making papier-mâché masks for the Day of the Dead. These activities prepared kids for neither college nor for careers in commercial art. Our new, leaner art department offered classes that included an element of art history. Eventually we added a section of advanced placement art.

We really gutted the home economics department. At one time we had one entire building full of stoves and sewing machines. Our girls were not gaining much knowledge in most of our home ec classes. They were not learning to cook gourmet meals or to design their own clothes. They were baking cookies with chocolate kisses in the middle. My daughter was doing that at home when she was ten. Most of our home ec students were cooking and sewing at home anyway. We needed money and space for remedial classes for students who were working well below grade level in their academic classes, and home ec was a luxury we could not afford at the time.

Not surprisingly many of the kids in home economics were poor academic performers who had been channeled into a lower track since middle school. They lost their electives to remedial reading and math classes, so they had no room in their schedules for home ec anyway. Eventually we got down to a single home economics teacher who taught five classes. When the time of mass remediation had ended, there was no groundswell of demand to restore home economics to its former size. Too many of our girls were making it in the academic track by then.

VOCATIONAL EDUCATION THAT IS STATE OF THE ART

If vocational education is not state of the art, it is not worth having. When I began at Garfield, our print shop was still using linotype, the method with letters molded from hot lead. There are no jobs for people with that skill, except maybe working in a museum demonstrating how printing was done decades ago. Students who wished to prepare for a career in printing were much better off taking a computer class, so we got rid of our print shop all together. When I first started at Garfield, our auto shop had the kids working on 1958 Chevies. There was not much point in that. It will not do kids much good to learn how to rebuild a carburetor when all the new cars have fuel injection.

In 1981 our star auto shop student took a job at a local mechanic's shop. By the end of the first day it was obvious that he could not continue to work there as a mechanic. What he knew did not apply to the modern vehicles that the shop was repairing. The owner let him stay on, but he just did menial, unskilled work like sweeping the floor. He worked alongside a recent immigrant from Mexico who had only attended school up to the sixth grade. They did the same work and received the same low pay. It was a disgrace that, after twelve years of school and three years of specialized vocational training, our student was only qualified for the same job and pay as someone who had only attended elementary school.

We cut back on the number of auto shop and other vocational offerings as we directed more kids into the academic track, but we used the savings to buy equipment that was state of the art. Our new, improved auto shop had computer diagnostic equipment, and the cars the kids worked on had fuel injection. Our drafting department was one of the few vocational programs that actually grew, but it changed substantially. We switched from pencil-and-paper drafting to computer-aided design. That was what employers wanted.

GAUGING THE SUCCESS OF A VOCATIONAL EDUCATION PROGRAM

A good gauge of the effectiveness of a vocational program is the average wage of its graduates. An auto shop graduate who can do little more than sweep the floor, mount tires, or fetch tools for the more skilled mechanics will never earn much more than minimum wage. By the late eighties we had a lot of voc-ed kids who were graduating from Garfield and moving into decent jobs. Some of our graduates who had studied computers got jobs as data entry specialists and started at $12 an hour, a very good starting wage back then. A lot of those kids eventually moved on to college.

We offered a semester-long floral arrangement class. The students who took that class were in great demand with area florists because they knew the basics. They knew the names of the flowers and how to arrange them. Those were skills the flower shops wanted. Our auto shop students were getting jobs as real mechanics because they knew how to work on the kinds of cars that were coming into the shops, not antiques that could only be found in junkyards and at classic auto shows.

SPECIAL EDUCATION THAT UPLIFTS RATHER THAN HOLDS BACK

The nature of special education has changed quite a bit since my time at Garfield. The Individuals with Disabilities Education Act, or IDEA law, was first enacted only a few years before my time at Garfield. It has since gone through a number of revisions. Back then, a lot of special education students were served on separate campuses, and we did not have the large number of students identified as learning disabled that most schools now do. As a result, we only had two special education teachers. Comparing special ed then and now is like comparing apples and oranges.

If the law as it exists today were in place in 1980, probably half of the kids coming into Garfield would have qualified for special education. Students whose academic performance is much lower than their IQ scores may now be labeled learning disabled and placed in a special education program. Since the average reading score of our entering sophomores was at one time more than four years below grade level, a lot of our students probably would have qualified if they had been tested.

A lot of our kids simply needed stronger courses and more demanding instruction than they had received in middle school. A great many responded to Garfield by rising to meet our expectations. It would have been a disgrace to shift these kids into special education simply because we could have. Still there are students who really cannot be held to the same standard as others. When this happens, there is a procedure to design curricula appropriate for special students with special needs.

THE DEADLY SERIOUS RESPONSIBILITIES OF THE IEP COMMITTEE

The IDEA law tells us to teach special education students in the least restrictive environment possible (LRE). When a student cannot succeed in school because of a disability, a committee creates an individual educational program, or IEP, which should be challenging yet attainable. The committee has a wide range of options, ranging from placement in a separate facility or self-contained classes on the home campus (most restrictive) to full mainstreaming with very limited monitoring (least restrictive).

The IEP committee has a tremendous responsibility. Sometimes an IEP simply mandates that a student will learn grade-level material in a different way, but sometimes it calls for different content or a different standard. The IEP committee has the power to give a student permission to learn less than other students are expected to learn. This is a responsibility to be taken very seriously. While we do not want to demand that a severely mentally challenged individual take higher math, neither do we want to make lesser demands on an individual who has the ability to succeed in such a class simply because of past failures or poor test scores.

APPROPRIATE PLACEMENT IN AND EXIT FROM SPECIAL EDUCATION

Students who can function in the mainstream should be there. The IEP specifies what can be reasonably expected of the students in whatever environment they are placed. Students who understand half of what they hear and read in regular academic classes probably are better off in the mainstream than they would be in very slow-paced remedial classes. The IEP committee can establish modifications and/or different performance standards for special students in the mainstream.

While I like mainstreaming very much, it is important to remember that the LRE is not always the regular classroom. If a student cannot stay in a seat for more than ten minutes, the least restrictive environment may be a special class where he or she can take frequent breaks without interrupting the educational process for all students.

The IEP should specify which behaviors result from the handicapping condition. A special education label is not permission to misbehave or to not advance academically. Special education students must understand that they are responsible for their actions unless those actions stem from their disability.

Special education placement can become both a self-fulfilling prophecy and an excuse to make a lesser effort. Too often, special education students label themselves. Teachers hear, "But I'm special ed" frequently. These students will benefit when they see themselves as part of the larger school community rather than part of a subgroup.

Many low-functioning students are capable of substantial improvement. It is not uncommon for low performers to improve two or more grade levels in a single year. Of course, this is not possible for all special education students, but it is for some. A successful special education program will eventually exit some of its students.

BILINGUAL AND ESL PROGRAMS

If a student does not know the language of the land, we have the obligation to prepare him or her to function and succeed in the English-speaking world. When I got to Garfield, we had a lot of high school kids who had been in bilingual education and ESL since preschool. That was definitely longer than necessary. We also had immigrant kids who had been in ESL for several years and still spoke English poorly. We looked for guidance to the Defense Language Institute (DLI), the school in Monterey, California, that trains language specialists for all branches of the military.

The DLI categorizes languages according to difficulty. Category I languages are those that are most similar to English, and therefore are the easiest for English speakers to learn. DLI allows six months for the study of a Cat I language like Spanish. Granted, DLI is selective, choosing students with a strong aptitude for languages, and students there study their target language full time. Still, we felt that, if DLI can get their students to function in a new language in six months, we should be able to get ours up to speed in eighteen.

English learners do not need a full native speaker's command of English to succeed in mainstream classes. A lot of the best graduate students at our top universities are foreign students who speak less than perfect English. An English learner with a limited but decent English vocabulary, other key English language skills, and the willingness to spend a lot of extra time looking up words from their textbooks can succeed in a regular content class.

A lot of English and Spanish words are cognates. Once Spanish speakers get used to English language sounds, it is easy for them to determine that *elephant* means *elefante* or that *planet* means *planeta.* An especially large percentage of science- and math-related words have Spanish cognates, so Spanish speakers who know these subjects already have a good head start.

Along with the ESL classes, we offered special content classes to our beginning ESL students. These classes were taught mostly in English, but the teachers were bilingual and translated expressions when appropriate. Each semester we looked at the kids' progress and determined appropriate placement in both ESL and content classes. Students who were still struggling after three semesters were placed in regular classes whether or not they felt that they were ready. I'm afraid that we had some who had to be pushed out of the nest, but we did not leave those students without support. Those who still needed more ESL were allowed to take an ESL support class as an elective for as many years as were necessary.

Unfortunately, many educators see ESL as some sort of a low group, and some ESL teachers are not as demanding as they should be. I found a lot of ESL teachers at Garfield were running their classes like elementary language arts. In order to be effective, ESL must be as demanding as any class offered at school. I encouraged the less-demanding ESL teachers to speed up their pace of instruction and push the kids harder. I am afraid that a lot of them decided that they would rather transfer to other district schools. When selecting new ESL teachers, I looked for those who were strong linguists and who spoke English well.

A lot of schools use the poor academic background of immigrant students as an excuse for failure. It is true that some immigrant kids come to this country with little prior education, but the number of those students is often exaggerated. A lot of our ESL students were both pretty sharp and well educated. Many of them had attended *escuela preparatoria*, or college prep high school, in Mexico. It is not unusual for former "*prepa*" students to have academic backgrounds as strong as or stronger than those of kids in honors classes in U.S. schools.

FIXING THE PROGRAM

We immediately removed the kids who had been in bilingual education and/ or ESL for five or more years. Those who had been in the program for three or four years were told that they would be allowed to take ESL for language arts credit for only one more semester. In many cases the elementary and middle schools had used limited English proficiency as an excuse for poor performance from kids who were actually English dominant.

The Limited English Proficient (LEP) label held these students in a program that did not benefit them in any way while masking other academic deficiencies that should have been addressed years before. If a school pretends that a poor reader is getting poor test scores because he or she does not speak English when that is not really the case, that student will not receive appropriate help.

Some of our ESL students were what linguists call semilingual. They were bilingual, but they did not speak either language like an educated native speaker. It is not that such students cannot communicate in English, but rather that they have not established an academe's command of either language. Such students are held back by studying, year after year, in classes that were designed for recent immigrants. Students do not learn academic English by studying the rudiments of a language they already speak fairly well. The place for such students is the mainstream, although backup remedial reading classes, tutoring, or other support may be appropriate.

I recall observing one of our American-born ESL students taking his annual test of oral English proficiency. He was being asked to describe pictures that he was shown. Although this test was appropriate for students who had only studied the English language for a short time, we were giving it to kids who had been in U.S. schools since kindergarten. When he was asked to describe a picture of a man getting off a bus, he said, "The dude's getting off the bus and some *vato*'s waiting to blow his a- - away." That kid belonged in the mainstream.

THE COST OF SUCCESS

By 1985 we had reduced the number of Garfield students in ESL classes from thirteen hundred to six hundred. Our success cost us a lot of money. The state provided $360 in extra funds for each student with the ESL label, so we lost about a quarter of a million bucks per year in ESL funding, but it was worth the monetary loss to more quickly move our LEP kids into the academic mainstream.

Scores on the CTBS and the CAP (California Academic Proficiency Test) indicated that we were successful. When Garfield LEP kids began to shine on standardized tests, the central office wanted to know the secret of our success. There were even some accusations that we were cheating. Our secret was simple. We taught them English.

The emphasis on English is in no way meant to disparage the students' native language. One way to help Spanish speakers maintain a sense of pride in their native language is to allow them to take and pass the AP Spanish test. The College Board does not require test takers to have taken the class. There is also an AP test in Spanish literature that many students who attended high school in Latin America could take, even if they did not study Spanish with us.

Chapter Eight

Physical Education, Sports, and Other Nonacademic Activities

When I began at Garfield I found that a lot of elements were out of balance: Vocational classes far outnumbered academic ones, basic classes outnumbered challenging ones, older teachers outnumbered younger ones, and male teachers greatly outnumbered female teachers by a factor of more than two to one. More than almost anything else, I found a lopsided emphasis on sports and other nonacademic activities.

I did not want to eliminate or even in any way disparage sports. It is certainly not that sports are bad. They are wholesome activities that provide participants with exercise, teach teamwork, and cause students and alumni to identify strongly with their school. They also create strong parental involvement. The problem was that in 1983 sports were the center of the Garfield universe. Academics were not even a distant second or third. Anyone could see that by simply looking at our yearbook. It contained little more than class photos and sports.

Early in my tenure as Garfield principal, we played football against Monroe High, a predominantly Anglo Los Angeles–area high school in the San Fernando Valley. While Monroe brought a respectable number of participants, our football team, band, and drill team were all more than three times the size of theirs. We had over one hundred kids who came to every varsity football game and suited up even though they had never played and never would. Varsity football was not really a participation sport for them. It was just a group that they got to belong to and identify with. Those kids were not succeeding at football, but they were not succeeding at much else either. Warming the benches gave them something to do on Friday nights, and being on the team provided them much-needed pats on the back.

When I visited Monroe, I saw why their team was so much smaller than ours. Like Garfield, Monroe had a full trophy case attesting to athletic accomplishment. Unlike Garfield's, Monroe's walls were covered with evidence of academic successes as well. There, sports and sports-related activities represented a small part of the whole. Monroe students had lots of accolades in lots of fields. They had winners in the academic decathlon, chess and debate championships, and numerous winners of prestigious scholarships.

At first I tried to shrink sports in order to foster academics. I now realize that that was a mistake. At that time Garfield had very little else to be proud of. It was not right to try to diminish football before we first supplemented it with something else.

A lot of our activities took place during the school day. Kids could take PE, varsity sports, band, *ballet folklorico*, or several other nonacademic activities for physical education credit. Some sports, like track, took place after school, but others, like football, basketball, and swimming, were assigned during sixth period, a time when other kids were taking academic classes. Some kids also got service credit, credit toward graduation, for helping in the office, kitchen, or library. Since our students were only required to take only one year of math and one of science, they had a lot of room in their schedules for these activities.

We decided that we had to cut nonacademic activities for kids with academic deficiencies. We denied extracurricular activities to students who did not maintain passing averages. Because we double-blocked classes for some of our students, we also sharply curtailed nonacademic curricular activities for students who were failing their classes and to entering sophomores who had poor math skills or who read below the seventh-grade level. Students who required remedial classes in two subjects lost out on all activities that took place during the school day.

We got some pretty strong reactions from the kids, the community, and even some of the faculty. Nothing gets people's attention like keeping a star athlete out of a game or suspending a senior cheerleader. The same happened with music. We had a kid come up from middle school who was a tremendous musical talent. As a boy in elementary school he played the coronet in his family's mariachi band and was known around East LA for his skill. The band director had been drooling in anticipation of his arrival at Garfield for years, but, when he got to us, he was not allowed to participate because he read far below grade level.

Remedial classes knocked him out of the band and music classes. There was a lot of gnashing of teeth over that situation. The boy, his parents, and the music teachers all came to me and begged me to bend the rules and let him join the marching band. I even got calls from the central office. I had to stand firm. If I let him join the band before he showed us that he could read at least at a seventh-grade level, we would have had to drop the standards for everybody.

As you might imagine, this boy, who had never really seen a reason to make a serious effort to learn how to read, suddenly found himself motivated to work hard to learn what he should have learned back in elementary school. Our remedial classes and our reading lab provided him the tools to learn, and the requirement that he attain a certain reading level in order to get his electives provided him a reason to do so. By the end of his third semester at Garfield, he was playing in the Bulldog marching band. He missed a year and a half of music, but he gained the literacy skills that he needed to really understand his high school textbooks.

Nobody stopped him from playing during that time. He practiced his music with his friends and his family, and he still performed at parties, *quinceañeras*, and various community events. When he finally was able to join our band he still had his musical touch. His parents, who had at first been angry at the time that he was excluded from the band, were delighted when they saw how he had progressed academically.

No Garfield extracurricular was hit harder than the pep club, which went from one hundred and fifty members to thirty-eight the first year that we instituted that no-pass-no-activity rule. The faculty sponsor was not very happy about the new situation. "You decimated our group," she told me. As our students began to take their studies more seriously, the number of students who were denied activities dropped. The pep club, however, never was restored to its former size. Many of those kids decided that they had better things to do.

At the same time that we cut back on the emphasis on sports, we pared back physical education. When I began at Garfield, all of our sophomores had to take PE. Some kids took PE every year, and varsity sports as well. California law required that all students have one year of physical education or sports during high school, but the law did not specify which year. The law also allowed students to take one semester of PE in each of two different years.

When kids came to us from the middle schools so low in academics that we had to double-block both language arts and math classes, there was no room in their schedules for PE. Those kids could take PE in their junior or senior years, after they mastered their basics well enough to enable them to benefit from their regular academic high school courses.

For some kids, varsity athletics took the place of PE, both in terms of credit and exercise. By the year 1985 we reduced the number of staff who exclusively coached and taught PE and health from ten down to five. The reduction in PE staff allowed us to add the staff we needed to teach our increasing number of academic classes. Of course, we still had a large number of coaches who also taught academic subjects.

My goal was not to eliminate activities, but to use them as a lever to help us achieve our main goal of preparing our students academically and to create a sensible balance. Unlike the earlier yearbooks that were plastered with sports and little else, the 1985 yearbook had a large academic section. By then, we were having rallies for everything that exhibited excellence. We even had rallies before our AP tests. Football remained important, but it was no longer *numero uno.*

The students and the community still came out to see the games, but students no longer moped for a week when we lost. We continued to field a decent team, but we did not have legions of kids who suited up and never played. They had other things to do. Our starters also had more in their lives than football. In 1986 the front line had an average grade point average (GPA) of 3.2, and all were taking at least one AP course.

Chapter Nine

Understanding and Controlling Gang Activity

In 1975, when I was a science and agriculture teacher at Garfield, our school had pretty much hit bottom. That year we had an accreditation evaluation. Usually, an accreditation team will give a school a dozen or so recommendations, but in 1975 Garfield received ninety-two. Gang activity had much to do with our condition. The school was controlled by eighteen different gangs then, each with a name and a specific area. As many as five hundred different kids were involved in those gangs. We had more kids in gangs than we did in college prep classes—a lot more.

The main eating area of the cafeteria was controlled by three of the larger gangs. Two gangs sat on opposite ends of the cafeteria and one sat in the middle on the far wall. Needless to say, the graffiti and the markings on the walls behind these "territories" were horrendous. The gangs intimidated the rest of the student body. Other students would pick up their food and leave the cafeteria because of the problems that occurred there.

Drugs were rampant: marijuana, uppers, downers, bennies, whites, reds, and a lot more. We had five security police and one female agent, and we kept a standby police car and a standby ambulance. Although Garfield was supposed to be a closed campus, kids came and left at will. Members of outside gangs visited the school and picked fights. Gang members congregated in the PE area and the rest rooms. The fights, the smell of marijuana, the sexual comments, and the gambling in the restrooms kept out the kids who came to Garfield to get an education.

We lived in fear of fights. Garfield lost a kid in 1971. He was being chased by a gang, and somebody threw a sharpened metal rod that hit him in the neck. He died before he hit the ground. Although the death did not occur on the Garfield campus, witnesses say that the lethal weapon was fashioned in our metal shop. No dress code was enforced. Students came in with tat-toos, hairnets, and other indicators of gang membership. Some wore serapes, turbans, or Indian garb. They claimed that the dress reflected their culture, but it was really to hide weapons.

The principal at that time had attempted to negotiate with the gangs. He put up boards where the gangs could draw their *placas*, or insignias, and allowed them to identify and claim gathering places. As you can imagine, the results were disastrous. Sometimes kids would cross out or deface the *placas* of rival gangs with graffiti, and that would lead to fights and beatings.

WHY SO MUCH GANG ACTIVITY?

Everyone likes to associate. That is human nature. We all congregate in groups, clubs, associations, cliques, and so on. We had a lot of such groups at Garfield, and not all of them were gangs. We had car clubs, groups of kids who liked to hang around together and fix up and customize automobiles, and we had the cliques and circles of friends common to all high schools. I myself was a member of my own gang of a sort, the circle of secondary school administrators.

When these associations do not have positive ends, there can be trouble. Our gang kids needed ways to distinguish themselves, so they resorted to a lot of negatives. In order to be recognized, they were willing to fight, defy authority, even to be arrested. In some ways, gang kids got treated like ESL or special education kids had been treated. When teachers tried to make academic demands, they often heard, "Hey, I'm gang," as though that alone was reason enough to not make a serious academic effort.

GANG BUSTING

We did not specifically set out to break up the gangs. We worked to eliminate negative behavior. A lot of that behavior came from gang members, and a lot of problems stemmed from gangs fighting over turf on our campus, so we had to keep track of who was in which gang. When I first came to Garfield, we had a Rolodex system. We took an ID picture as part of registration. We made four prints: one went on the ID card, one went to the counselor, one went to the assistant principal, and one went to the dean of discipline. I kept a Polaroid camera in my office and, when students registered late, we took a picture on the spot.

Some of our gang problems came from kids who were not even enrolled at Garfield. Sometimes gang kids would walk onto campus and lurk in the halls. Some were homies just wanting to hang out, and some were outside kids coming to school specifically looking for trouble. We dealt with this problem by controlling access to the school. We locked unmanned gates, and we had someone at all accessible doorways during school hours. Any Garfield student who came through those gates after school had begun had to go to the auditorium or office and go through the tardy procedures described in chapter 4. Any nonstudents with school business had to first go to the office and then were directed or escorted to their destinations. Nonstudents who had no good reason to be on campus were denied access.

A lot of gang problems that happened in the streets spilled over into Garfield. Sometimes a fight that began Saturday night somewhere on Whittier Boulevard or elsewhere in East LA would be continued in Garfield. I asked the police to give me a blotter every Monday morning so we could take steps to keep these fights from reigniting in our halls.

We never had a strict dress code, but we did ban clothing that could conceal weapons. We stopped allowing kids to wear "fashion accessories" like chains that were heavy enough to be used as weapons. Caps with insignias and other articles of clothing that were identified with specific gangs were also prohibited.

Winning kids away from the gang culture and into a positive school culture is a long, slow process. In the short run, the only way to control gangs is to enforce the rules. When the penal code was violated, we called law enforcement. By my second year as principal at Garfield, we had an iron-clad no fighting rule. Again, I did not get involved in penal matters involving drug possession and assault. When parents came to me to complain, I told them to take the matter up with the police.

DISRUPTING GANG MEMBERSHIP

The worst thing that can happen to a gang is to lose its membership. When a gang member repeatedly violated school rules or was arrested for violating the penal code, I did not let him back on campus. After the courts finished with him, he was transferred to another school. We also transferred out kids for repeated lesser gang-related activities. If we caught a kid tagging once, he would be suspended. After three incidences of tagging, he was out of Garfield. I had to stand firm on this matter. More than once, I had to tell central office administrators, "If this kid's at Garfield next week, I won't be."

A lot of principals are too timid to make such a call, but they should not be. No judge is going to put a restraining order on a principal. Gangs are turf-based, and gang members, especially gang leaders, do not want to cross several other gangs' turf on their way to a school where they have no power base. After having their leaders transferred out, many of these gangs fell apart. Members of those that did not at least learned the importance of keeping a low profile while they were on campus.

We did not have to transfer that many kids. Even the threat of a transfer was daunting for these gang kids. They did not want to be taken off of their turf. The first time a gang kid got into any sort of trouble, I would call him into my office and fill out transfer papers right in front of him, filling in everything except the date. I would tell him that the transfer would become active the next time he got into any kind of trouble, and then I would give the student a copy to carry around as a reminder. This technique worked.

We once had a faceoff in the halls between two students who were leaders of rival gangs. After a verbal altercation, the first pulled out his unsigned transfer form and shouted, "The only thing that keeps me from killing you is this piece of paper!" The other student responded by showing him his own transfer form and saying, "This is the only reason I don't kick your a--!" Kids like these felt that they had an obligation to fight. If they were leaders, the lower-level gang members expected them to do battle with leaders of rival gangs. The transfer threat gave them an excuse to not fight, or at least not fight on my turf, Garfield High School.

TRANSFERRING TO OTHER TURF

Student transfer was a two-way street. We could not send our gang students to other LAUSD schools unless we were willing to accept theirs. This was not necessarily a negative experience for the student. Some of the transfer kids did drop out, but they were kids who were not interested in studying anyway. Some students found transfers both into and out of Garfield to be an opportunity to start fresh.

A standout among students who transferred into Garfield because of gang activity was Martin Herrera, who came to us from another LAUSD high school. He had been wounded in a gang-related drive-by shooting in which one of his friends was killed. He got involved in the math enrichment program, eventually took calculus, and passed the AP exam. After graduation he entered the University of California, Santa Barbara and went on to teach high school math.

FILLING THE VOID

Some of these kids joined gangs because they did not have much else in their lives. We did what we could to make gang kids want to identify themselves as Garfield students rather than gang members. I put gang kids in charge of graffiti control. I had them paint murals and get involved in community service. We had *cholos* and *pachucos* delivering groceries to East LA senior citizens.

We had to show them that, by sticking to legitimate organizations, groups, and clubs, and by being academically wise, they could get extreme recognition and feel better about themselves without the negative consequences that result from illegal activities. They needed to understand that they could get a bigger high by being a member of the chess club and defeating another school, by excelling in sports, or by earning a scholarship to a major university than by vandalizing a building at night.

A lot of the gang kids are pretty sharp. A kid has to have something on the ball to stay a step ahead of the police. The character Angel in *Stand and Deliver* was very loosely based on Armando Islas, a real Escalante student. Islas had been a gang member while in middle school and has the knife scars to prove it. His life while he was a student at Garfield was different.

He was not actively involved in gang activity at the time he was taking the calculus class. He did not have obscenities tattooed on his knuckles, nor did he throw tantrums in class like the character in the film. In fact, Escalante's biggest complaint about him was that baseball was cutting into his study time. He really did ask Escalante for an extra textbook so his homies would not see him carrying a math textbook home. That former student is now a Harvard graduate, a dentist, a surgeon, and an exporter of medicine and medical equipment.

Some of the gang kids were good kids who joined up in middle school because they were afraid not to. They lived on the gang's turf and got swept up in gang activity. Many of them were on the fringes of gang life. They were not enthusiastic about gang life, but they did get called on to participate in gang activities, including the illegal ones. Sometimes I talked to the gang leaders about leaving certain kids alone.

I explained that a certain kid was on his way to becoming a doctor, and that he would be coming back to the barrio some day to help his people. He did not need gang activity getting in the way. Sometimes the gang leaders would listen. Kids like these were the greatest beneficiaries of the weakening of the gangs' grip on Garfield.

A lot of the kids understood that the gang life was not the good life. Some kids felt that gang membership was the only way to protect themselves in a hostile environment. Once we established order and safety at Garfield, kids had one less reason to get involved in gangs. Before being led out of Garfield for the last time, one gang member hugged me and asked me to talk to his mother. Another, who had been removed from Garfield a few years before, approached me outside of school and asked me to keep my eye on his little brother.

Not everyone understands. I attended many student funerals in my years as an educator. I once attended the funeral of a former Garfield student who I had one month before transferred out for assaulting another student. His mother graciously thanked me for attending and for a contribution I made toward a memorial, but his younger brother was angry with me and demanded to know how I could attend his brother's funeral after I had forced him to leave Garfield, his home turf. I had to explain that it was not personal. I was fond of his brother, but he would not conform to Garfield's rules, so he had not been allowed to stay.

I grew up in East LA around the gang culture, I worked with gang kids for much of my career, and I have learned that gang kids do have a certain sense of honor, albeit a distorted one. Gang kids understand the concept of rules, and some of their own rules can be pretty severe. In the gang world the penalty for violating them can be death. It is important to be straight with gang kids. Cooking up false charges to justify removing gang members is not necessary. Kids who repeatedly break the rules will get caught soon enough.

When we started the tardy sweeps, the majority of the kids we picked up were in gangs. After several violations of our attendance rules, we had justification to take punitive action. Much of our drug activity and most of our fights were gang related. Kids who fought or carried drugs got caught sooner or later. Kids at Garfield understood that anyone guilty of these offenses would be gone immediately. I told them, "I'm not after you because you're gang, but you are going to have to conform or leave." Word got out in the gang community that Gradillas was not anti-gang or anti-anything, but he was fair.

It is important that gang kids know that the people running their schools respect them, but that the rules are for everyone, and that those who would not follow them would experience consequences. The adults ran the school, not the gangs. That is how we took away their turf. I told the kids, "This turf belongs to me." In their own way, most of them respected that. I never hid my address. It was listed in the phone book. I often went into gang neighborhoods to visit students' homes. Sometimes I personally delivered turkeys at Thanksgiving or gifts at Christmas to homes in neighborhoods with high gang activity.

Sometimes gang kids would confront me, and once in a while I'd be asked, "You packing heat, Gradillas?" I never was. If I had been, I would have been fair game. My response was always, "My weapon is my pen. I can use it to sign your diploma, or I can use it to sign your transfer." When I left Garfield six years later, the number of viable gangs was down to three, and the gang culture that had once prevailed had virtually disappeared.

Chapter Ten

Selecting, Supervising, and Supporting the Teaching Staff

No school can be successful without good teachers. The best school climate, the best facilities and materials, the most competent administrators, and the most demanding curriculum will not make a school effective unless there are competent people on the front lines. It is essential to hire, support, and retain good people in the classrooms.

TEACHER SELECTION

Once a teacher has been accepted as a member of the teaching staff, the influence that teacher will have on the entire school and community will be felt in many ways for years to come, in many cases years beyond the principal's tenure. For this reason the best and most qualified teachers must be chosen through a well-thought-out selection process.

When I began at Garfield, teacher selection was not really an issue. We usually had to take whomever we could get. We began my first year as principal at Garfield short ten certified teachers. Not many teachers volunteered for Garfield, and some of those whom the personnel office assigned to teach there simply chose not to show up. Sometimes my only choices were to accept the sole candidate or leave the class in the hands of a long-term substitute. It was not until my third year that we were able to start really choosing our staff. By the fourth year Garfield's improved reputation enabled us to actually become selective.

When I was at Birmingham we had site-based administration, so we were obliged to go through a committee when we selected new staff. There were no such requirements at Garfield in the eighties, but I found it wise to involve staff in hiring. Usually the selection committee included at least the department chair, assistant principals, and the head counselor.

At Garfield we had two parent advisory councils, a Chapter I council and a bilingual/ESL council. These councils were made up of and were elected by community members. Advisory council members were involved in the selection of teachers involved in those programs. Even when they were not directly involved in selection, we sought their input.

GOING TO THE TREE

I found that the worst thing that I could do was to wait for Downtown (LAUSD slang for the central office) to send teacher candidates to us. Personnel was not about to send its best and brightest candidates to the East LA barrio. In order to get the best possible candidates, we had to bypass the personnel offices and recruit for ourselves. USC, UCLA, and Cal State LA all sent student teachers to us. At first the numbers were low.

The education professors told us that nobody wanted to student teach at Garfield. After Garfield's reputation improved, we were able to attract several, especially in math. A lot of student teachers wanted to work in Escalante's program. Student teachers had an opportunity to observe and work with our teachers for an entire semester, and they had an opportunity to get a feel for Garfield, and our teachers were able to observe them on the job and determine whether or not to recommend them for regular positions.

USC had a program that prepared and credentialed degreed adults with experience working outside of education. I was fortunate to be on the selection committee for that program. When I saw promising candidates, I invited them to visit our campus and to consider applying for a position there. Sometimes I had the opportunity to address students at colleges of education. Whenever I did, I included a sales pitch for Garfield.

Our teachers were also very helpful. I asked teachers to tell me when they planned to retire or transfer so that we could start looking for replacements as soon as possible. The union was very helpful in this matter. I would then ask my staff to recommend teachers, or to help recruit teachers for me.

DESIRABLE QUALITIES OF TEACHERS

Four main qualities are critical to teacher success:

Knowledge of the Subject Taught

Knowledge of the subject taught stands out as the most important prerequisite for teaching secondary school. I have known teachers who had wonderful people skills and even exceptional classroom management skills, but who were weak in their knowledge of their subjects. In some cases, their students were happy and their classrooms were orderly, but little learning was taking place under their watch. They were great day-care providers, but pretty ineffective teachers. Teachers who have a narrow preparation in their chosen fields short their students. Teachers need to have broad backgrounds in their fields in order to bring depth to their teaching and to be able to reach all or most of their class members.

I have seen teachers whose minimal knowledge barely allowed them to keep a page or two ahead of the curriculum. Teachers who see a spark of interest in some kids should have the knowledge necessary to fan that spark into a flame. During Escalante's first year at Garfield, when he was teaching basic math, he was able to convince several of his students to study algebraic concepts that were way beyond the basic math curriculum. Later on, he was able to plant the seeds that helped interest his students in higher math. If those kids had had a teacher whose knowledge of math was only a page or two ahead of the general math curriculum, Garfield's history would have been different.

Administrators, department chairs, and mentoring teachers can often share teaching methods and classroom management techniques on the job, but they cannot teach novice teachers subject matter that they were unable to master in four or more years of college. When Escalante was building his math dynasty, he asked me to hire people with very strong knowledge of their subjects. He did a great job of preparing teachers who taught the classes that led up to calculus and calculus itself.

Two standout teachers who had learned teaching techniques from Escalante were Ben Jimenez and Angel Villavicencio. Like Escalante, Jimenez taught calculus during Garfield's AP calculus glory years, and had an AP passing rate every bit as high as Escalante's. Villavicencio, who taught calculus feeder classes when Escalante and Jimenez taught calculus, took over calculus at Garfield after Escalante left and did an admirable job. He later went on to build an extremely successful AP calculus program in Chino, California. Although they both learned a lot from Escalante, both had very solid understandings of their subjects before they began teaching.

Passion for the Sharing of Knowledge

Beyond knowledge, it is important to have a passion for the subject taught and a burning desire to share that knowledge. Angel Villavicencio explained it well when he said, "The classroom is the temple, math is the religion, and

I'm the priest." That kind of enthusiasm is contagious. Passionate teachers live to see students learn. Nothing excites them more than to see students catch their enthusiasm. Such teachers tend to be demanding, since they know that knowledge is a worthy goal, more important than student self-esteem or anything else that might be gleaned from their classes.

Experience

Experience in teaching children and young adults is of great importance. If we were fortunate enough to have applicants with successful teaching experience, we were happy to get them on board, but many applicants who had work experience outside of education or who just came to us from the university had applicable experience as well. People who had been in management positions in business or leadership positions in the military have much to bring to teaching.

With recent graduates, we liked to see experience as tutors or teaching assistants. Novice teachers who had volunteered to work in literacy programs in college were also welcome. After Escalante's program had been well established, we got applicants who had been his student tutors or teaching assistants while still in high school and others who had volunteered while studying at USC, UCLA, or Cal State.

Willingness to Go Beyond the Minimum

Willingness to participate in extracurricular activities is another important consideration in teacher selection. It is a good idea to allow a teacher new to a school to have a few semesters to acquaint himself or herself with the profession, the school, and the community before taking on extra responsibilities, but a willingness to be a club or class sponsor, activities director, tutor, or mentor must be ascertained. Teacher burn-out among experienced staff can be a problem. Not every teacher possesses Escalante's energy.

Sometimes good older teachers would tell me that they no longer had the energy to teach a full load and sponsor three or four activities, or that health problems or family commitments forced them to slow down. Sometimes teachers just need a break for a year or two. It is hard to deny a break to a workhorse who has given his or her spare time to the yearbook, the choir, or athletics for twenty-five years. I could look in our yearbooks and see that some of these teachers had been shouldering extra-curricular burdens for decades. Sometimes the need was not immediate, but it is always good to know that staff will be available when the need arises.

I also wanted all of my new teachers to be willing to eventually teach honors or advanced placement courses. Even if only a few students in the school have sufficient background to take AP classes at the time of the hiring, having teachers on the staff who are willing and able to teach these classes gives the school room to grow. Garfield could not have gone from one to seventeen sections of chemistry if we had not had enough staff qualified to teach the growing number of students who had become well-enough prepared to take it.

GAINING TRUST AND KEEPING FAITH

It is very important to win and keep the trust of the teachers. I could understand why some Garfield teachers were reluctant to support me when I started as principal there. Garfield had had five principals in ten years, and a lot of teachers had been burned before by administrators who had spoken of high standards but turned tail when students, parents, or administrators from the central office started complaining.

It was not the inexperienced or poor-performing teachers who were expressing their concerns, but the best ones I had, teachers who sincerely wanted to teach. Although I had more often than not gotten the support of the union, the union reps were also gun-shy. They told me to go slowly, that the new changes were more than people were ready for.

A lot of teachers wanted the same things that I wanted but were afraid that I would not follow through. One told me, "If Downtown offers you an area superintendency in a year or two, you'll be out of here, we'll be working for someone who wants to go back to the way things were, and everyone who did things your way will be on the s--- list." Some staff members trusted my intentions, but not my ability to deliver. Our librarian, said, "If you self-destruct by having the central office remove you from your principalship because of your tactics, Garfield is going to be worse than it was before because they'll send in someone who will bend to the pressures."

A science teacher, a friend of mine from my teaching days, very articulately said, "You promised to support us. If you really mean it, we will support you, but, if we expose our soft underbellies by following your lead and you back down (to the central administration, parents, Mexican Commission, local and state officials, etc.), and our bellies get cut, we're going back to the status quo."

Promises were not enough. The teachers had heard enough of them. I had to show them that I would deliver. When I told biology teachers to add more lab activities, they told me that they needed more frogs. If I did not deliver them the teachers would have known that I was all talk and no action. When I asked teachers to assign homework, we had to have a system in place that supported the teachers when students came to class empty-handed.

When I demanded order and respectful behavior in the classes and the halls, the administration had to provide support to teachers whose students flaunted their rules. When I asked for high academic standards, we had to support teachers when students and parents complained about poor grades and high failure rates. As far as providing enough time to turn the school around, I promised that I would stay five years before seeking a promotion. I ended up staying six.

SUPERVISING TEACHERS

Teachers take a lot of the blame for problems in schools. A number of parents and fellow administrators suggested that I start by eliminating the poorer teachers. Again, trying to first correct instruction before establishing a positive school climate kills any chance of creating an effective school. An otherwise competent administrator I know failed to survive at his high school because his approach was to hit the teachers first.

No administrator can raise test scores by first attacking the delivery of instruction. In the first place, this approach gives the kids the impression that they are off the hook, that they are not responsible for anything that goes on in their school. In the second place, this tactic will cause the teachers to buck the administration from day one. Everybody loses when that happens.

I cannot stress too much that, if a school is in near-total disarray, a principal might need to spend a lot of time, perhaps as much as the entire first year, working on school climate before zeroing in on instruction. However, if there are teachers who are hopelessly below standard, who flagrantly violate the rules, or who refuse to even attempt to provide meaningful instruction, they must be dealt with immediately.

Even in the climate-building stage, a principal cannot tolerate teachers who make sexually explicit remarks, come to school under the influence of alcohol, come totally unprepared for the day's instruction, or put their feet up and read the newspaper while the students mindlessly copy text or chat among themselves. Marginal teachers, however, should be dealt with later. It is essential to first establish order and build morale. This way, principals will get the support of most of the teachers before they start picking at the weakest of them.

MONITORING INSTRUCTION

At least by the second year, when a principal needs to focus on instruction, the supervision of instruction needs to be on a continual basis. Early in the instruction-building phase, principals need to almost live in the classrooms to see the way that instruction is occurring. It's extremely important to be where instruction is delivered and to talk to the teachers regularly.

MONITORING GRADES

I was not one of those principals who would pressure teachers into changing grades or softening their grading policies. Grading was the teachers' domain, and the kids and their parents had to understand that teachers' grades were inviolate. I could not ask my teachers to hold the kids to tough standards and then back off at report card time. When we first required algebra for all students, some of our teachers reported an 80 percent failure rate. We had to live with that for a time. I did, however, ask the teachers to explain the reasons for high failure rates. I did not accept, "They're poor, they're Latino," and so forth.

If the reason was that the kids were unprepared for the class, we got them into a double-blocked class that offered remedial help. If the reason was that the students were not doing their homework, I did not go after the teachers; I went after the kids, even if it meant chastising 90 percent of the class. I would call kids into the auditorium, contact the parents, sic the counselors on them, assign Saturday classes, write contracts—whatever it took.

In LAUSD semesters were twenty weeks long. There are four reporting periods in each semester. At the end of the first and the third reporting periods, we issued failure notices only. The second and fourth, we issued actual grade reports. Students who were failing more than two classes after the second reporting period were called into the auditorium and were given a warning. Those who were still failing after the third were denied permission to participate in extra-curriculum activities. If the failures were in core classes, the students were assigned Saturday classes or were pulled out of a nonacademic elective and were placed in a remedial class for the duration of the semester.

THE GREEN LIGHT

Sometimes the best thing an administrator can do is just get out of the way. If teachers are strong, administrators need to respect that strength and allow them a great deal of autonomy. Escalante used to brag that he had the green light. I did not have to check to know that he was in MH 1 teaching his heart out. I just gave him all the building keys he wanted, supported him in every way that I could, and let him do what he loved to do.

SUPPORTING TEACHERS

All administrators have to understand that they have very little control over what happens in the classroom after the teacher closes the door. It is impossible to micromanage the classroom from the office. If administrators are going to have input in instruction, there must be give and take between the administration and the teaching staff. Administrators have the right and the responsibility to demand that teachers do what the taxpayers pay them to do, but it is hard to make demands on teachers if the administration is not providing them with good working conditions.

There are many ways that administrators can support their teachers. The kids need to understand that they are to treat all staff members with respect. Staff members need to know that when there is a matter they cannot handle alone they can and should report it, and that they can count on getting support. There are, unfortunately, administrators who deal with problems by kicking them back to the teachers.

If I demanded that teachers assign meaningful homework and then refused to take action when a teacher sent me a student who had not turned in any homework in the past two weeks, the teacher would figure, "Why bother?" and drop standards. If teachers are blamed for all the problems they report, they learn not to report them. They then will keep the problems in the classroom where they will, like mushrooms, grow in the dark.

Another way to support teachers is to back them when parents complain. A lot of parental complaints had to do with poor grades. I did ask that teachers keep good records. On the occasion that a bad grade was the result of teacher error, I expected the teacher to apologize and move on. When the teachers had all the ducks in a row, as was usually the case, we backed them 100 percent. When I supported teachers in grading matters, everyone realized that grades meant something.

We supported teachers in matters of discipline. Teachers were expected to enforce their own classroom rules. If a teacher chose to ban gum, that was the teacher's choice. But we had a list of violations that had to be reported to the administration. Penal code violations were reported to the police, and then passed out of our hands. Chronic tardies were an administrative matter that we would handle.

If a teacher assigned consequences like detentions or additional tasks and the student refused to comply, the office would take the next necessary step. Teachers were required to report all fights, to tell the belligerents to stop fighting, and to call security or an administrator as soon as possible, but they were not required to attempt to physically break up the fight. I never ordered my teachers to put themselves in harm's way.

Field trips were considered a privilege. When students went on all-day field trips, all of their teachers had to sign a permission slip. Any teacher could deny the privilege to a student who was behind in assignments or who had not been behaving well. If a teacher did so, there was no appeal to the administration. The teacher's decision always stood in this matter.

Toward the end of my tenure at Garfield, we started scheduling classes for the following year in the spring before school let out. After the last final exam was given, we scheduled a preview day in which kids would report to the classes that they would be attending the following year. Of course, we couldn't schedule all of the kids since we had a number of transfers, but we could schedule most of them. Teachers appreciated this small courtesy because it allowed them to plan during the summer. Teachers could also provide students a syllabus with recommended or required reading lists, or set up preview sessions for the summer.

MATERIAL SUPPORT

Administrators can support their staffs by getting teachers items that they need for the classroom. I have found that very few requests from teachers are unreasonable. Usually their requests are for things that improve instruction. Obviously, finite funding means that not everyone can get everything they want all at once, but many requests can be granted. When I first met with my teachers, I handed out note cards and asked them to answer three questions: What can I, as a principal, get you right now? What can I get you in several months? What is your wish list? Some requests were as simple as fixing a lock or replacing a defective piece of equipment.

It is important for administrators to understand what their teachers are doing as well as their teaching styles. This helps administrators understand what teachers most need in order to prioritize requests. A physics teacher wanted drapes to make his room dark enough for experiments with light and lasers. An anthropology teacher wanted a room-sized rug. He taught a comparative religion class and brought in representatives from many religious groups to speak, and it worked well for him to have his students sit on the floor while they listened.

Escalante wanted recently published calculus books and a larger blackboard so he could leave his notes up for a few days. When his popularity grew, he asked for a room large enough to accommodate all of the students who wanted to take his class. The following year, I got him the famed MH1, a former band hall that could seat seventy. I later got MH2, a similar room, for his fellow calculus teacher, Ben Jimenez.

Sometimes principals can get these items by doing some horse swapping with other principals or by personally bugging someone in the central office. I sometimes delivered equipment personally in my own pickup rather than make teachers wait for later scheduled deliveries. Gestures like these build good will and make it easier to get teachers to volunteer time or to go above and beyond the minimum required of them.

Some administrators actually accused me of spoiling my teachers. As a result of Garfield gaining a reputation as a good place to work, we suddenly began getting several applicants for each position, and we then had the option of choosing from a pool of well-qualified individuals instead of scraping for enough certified or emergency-credentialed teachers to fill our rosters as we had a few years earlier.

THE CARROT AND THE STICK

We did have some teachers who were not performing up to the standards that I expected. I did not want to be punitive, but some teachers had to shape up or ship out. Once principals have observed and supervised instruction, they will understand some of the problems that occur in their classrooms. At that point, they must let teachers know if they are performing poorly. They can have meetings with the teachers who are struggling, offer them meaningful inservices, or give them released time to observe a master teacher, either on their campus or another. They can pair novice teachers with strong role models or assign mentoring teachers.

Department chairs can be helpful in mentoring weak teachers. At Garfield our department chairs were given additional conference periods and, in some cases, stipends. We considered mentoring to be part of their jobs. Department chairs cannot evaluate teachers. That is the administrators' job. They can, however, help teachers. They can observe, call meetings, review lessons plans, and advise. They are not there to appraise, but rather to assist.

A lot of our teachers were pretty good about helping novices out without being asked by their superiors and without asking anything in return. Sometimes I would ask a veteran teacher to help out a novice. If I did, I was willing to offer some favor in return. One of my teachers was not always able to get her children to elementary school and still get to Garfield in time for her first-period class. I gladly gave her a first period conference and allowed her to come in late, but I asked her to make up that time by helping out a new teacher who was having problems.

Chapter Eleven

Winning Over the Kids

If a school is to be effective, the students and the staff have to be on the same side. It is important to remember that there must be a positive school climate before a school can be successful, and that school climate falls heavily on the kids. The kids outnumber the staff, and there is a lot that they can do to get back at teachers and administrators. They can stay home, disrupt classes, or even vandalize cars. Teachers and administrators need the support of the majority of the kids. This creates a problem in a school like the Garfield High of the early eighties. To both get and maintain control of the school and to win over the kids, I had to be hardnosed, but not an SOB.

Most of the students want what teachers and administrators want, a safe, orderly environment where learning takes place. If you look at the total numbers of serious offenders in any school, even the toughest ones, you will find that the percentage of students who deal and use drugs, vandalize school property, get involved in gang activity, and start fights is low. Probably more than most kids, minority kids either openly or tacitly wish that their schools were more orderly and their teachers more demanding than they actually are.

It is surprisingly easy for administrators to get the support of most students when they crack down on serious offenses. The general school population will be grateful when the worst of the problems get cleaned up. Most kids do not want to attend a dirty school, nor do they want to share their classrooms and hallways with kids who terrorize their classmates.

A lot of kids actually fled Garfield in the seventies. In order to get away from those elements, some families that could afford to move to places with better schools did so. Some kids actually moved or pretended to move in with relatives who lived in different attendance zones or school districts. Many kids who lived in Garfield's attendance zone enrolled in area Catholic schools even though this often represented a huge financial burden for their families.

A lot of people would be surprised to hear the reaction immigrant kids had to some of our inner-city schools. When these kids come across the border they expect to see a brighter world than the one they left, but it does not always work that way. Imagine coming to what you think is the land of milk and honey and finding yourself in a barrio or ghetto school where the walls are covered with graffiti, the toilets do not work, and teenage gangs rule the halls.

When I was still a teacher at Garfield, a recent immigrant from Mexico City told me that the school she came from was one hundred times better than the one she attended now. She added, "And you call us the third world." There is really no excuse for this to be the case. With our wealth and re-sources, and with the amount of money dedicated to education in the United States, we can afford to have good schools, but the right elements have to be in place.

THE POWER OF A CLEAN, SAFE RESTROOM

When I started at Garfield, half of the restrooms were permanently locked. Previous administrations had closed them because of vandalism, fights, as-saults, and drug use. They left open only the bathrooms that the staff could actively monitor. The bathrooms that remained open were in disrepair. There were no mirrors because vandals kept shattering them. Even the girls' toilet stalls lacked doors. Sanitary napkin vending machines usually did not work because they were always being broken into.

I had a private restroom near my office, and sometimes kids would ask if they could use it. A lot of the kids were afraid to go into the student rest-rooms between classes because of the activity there. Sometimes there would be drug use, or kids would be shaken down for their pocket change. This created problems for teachers as well. Kids would ask for restroom passes during class time either because they felt safer then or else because between classes the lines were too long in our remaining open restrooms. It also created potential heath problems, since some kids would avoid our restrooms all day and try to wait until they got home before relieving themselves.

I could not have immediately opened all of the restrooms even if I had wanted to. Some of the vandalized facilities had not been repaired, and the locked restrooms had been cannibalized over the years. When school plum-bers needed to replace a sink or commode, they just took one from a sealed restroom.

This was a marvelous opportunity to get kids involved in taking care of their own school. Early in 1981 I called the kids into the auditorium for the first of what the kids came to call my daddy talks. I explained that the students had a right to clean, functioning bathrooms. I planned to open the closed restrooms, one at a time. I would also order mirrors and the doors on the toilet stalls replaced in the girls' restrooms that were still open, but that I would need their help. We assigned staff members to check out the restrooms when they had time, but we obviously could not have teachers stationed there all the time. If the students were to have clean, functioning restrooms, they had to do their part.

I assured the student body that anyone who was caught vandalizing a restroom, extorting money from other students, or otherwise making kids afraid would be transferred out immediately. I asked that anyone with information about students misusing the facilities inform a staff member immediately. Of course, we would accept anonymous tips. This would not be something that the students would do for me. I had my own clean, safe bathroom. This was something that they would do for their own benefit. Nobody cheered or clapped, but I could sense silent approval. After the restrooms were repaired and renovated, we still had some minor problems. We did have to replace a few mirrors and a few stall doors, but the kids got the message. Kids came by the office or notes appeared in my mailbox after acts of vandalism were committed.

I knew that the kids were taking responsibility for their own restrooms because daily inspections revealed little vandalism. Four Garfield girls caught a recent transfer student tagging a restroom and escorted her to my office with the remarks, "This girl was marking up our restroom, and we want her out. You promised us that, if we would help you, you would keep the restrooms clean." I cancelled her permit and she was transferred back to her home campus. The girls who reported the incident even asked for cleaning supplies and a bit of time to clean up.

We also had to help the kids take back their cafeteria. During my first semester as principal at Garfield, we had a major food fight at least once a week. For several years, our cafeteria had not served whole pieces of fruit because fruit so often had been used as projectiles. We had a special cutter that quartered apples and oranges so that we could serve them in a less dangerous form. The more powerful gangs had staked out corners of the cafeteria and made them off limits to the regular kids. A lot of the kids picked up their food and left the cafeteria as quickly as possible because they knew there would be problems there.

We put in strict rules about misbehavior in the cafeteria. About 95 percent of our kids received subsidized breakfast and lunch. I told the kids that anyone involved in a food fight would either be denied free lunch or else be obliged to eat in a separate room under close faculty supervision. If parents came in to complain, I would ask them to sit with their kids and supervise them while they ate. Most of the kids appreciated getting their cafeteria back. One of the last food fights we had at Garfield ended when most of the kids sitting at the offending tables turned their backs on the kids who were fighting.

The young Hispanic community does not like tattletales. Kids knew that any information I received would be 100 percent confidential. Once, a student had information that a kid had a bayonet. He walked by me in the cafeteria and said, "Hi, Mr. Principal," shook my hand, and left in it a piece of paper saying "---- has a bayonet. He flashed it this morning." It was signed "anonymous." I told kids they had a responsibility to report weapons.

If a student has a weapon and uses it, someone will be hurt, and the perpetrator will be in worse trouble than he would have been simply for possession. The main thing is to remove the dangerous object. The law will be involved if a kid has a weapon, but the charge will be less than murder. The student community began to understand that it is better to remove the object that might get someone into serious trouble.

In 1983 we had an evening dance. There was an argument between two members of different gangs, and the argument led to a fight. One kid kicked in a bass drum. We stopped the dance and sent everybody home. Some kids asked for their money back, but the admission price was not returned. The next day I talked to the kids. Some asked me why I let the troublemakers in. Some of them were not even Garfield students.

I did not know who the troublemakers were, but some of the kids did. I asked for their help. I needed to have potential troublemakers identified so my staff could keep an eye on them. I needed help moving the chronic troublemakers out. I asked kids to bring me information, and I asked them to talk to their parents about supporting me in moving trouble-making kids out. The kids came forward with the information I needed.

We had one student who had been in the penal system who was to be released to Garfield on a minute order, a judicial writ ordering a student to attend a certain school as a condition of parole or probation. Several kids approached me about this one. The grapevine reported that he had already committed a gang-related murder for which he had not been charged or arrested, that he would be gunning for some Garfield kids, and that, if he were to come to Garfield, we could count on bloodshed. I had to lock horns with a judge on that one. I ended up offering to take some other parolees on other minute orders, but that this one would have to go elsewhere. The judge finally concurred. One of the gang leaders told me, "I owe you one, Gradillas."

We made the daddy talks regular events. We always had them at the beginning of each semester and at other important times. When there was an important event in the offing, or something with a significant impact, like a death in the community, students reported to the auditorium. Student response to the assemblies was good and improved with each semester during the first few years.

GETTING HELP FROM STUDENT LEADERS

We asked the student council and the class officers to help us out. At one time the student council at Garfield was a joke. They oversaw the yearbook, organized a few activities, and made occasional statements, but they were not taken very seriously. At the same time, their peers in more affluent LAUSD schools had more serious roles. We sought the same for ours.

We invited our student council members into some of our administrative and faculty meetings, we welcomed their input, and we seriously considered that input when we made policies. In exchange, we asked for help in gathering student support for those policies. Each month we had student council members address the student population either at assemblies or in the classrooms.

Our kids really wanted some of what students in more prosperous schools take for granted. Clubs would do student exchanges with other LAUSD schools. Representatives of student government spent time meeting with their peers on other campuses and they would observe classes and activities there. Some would return wondering why our campus couldn't look like the ones they had visited. I told them that I would do what I could to make that possible, if they would help out.

We wanted the kids to understand how important it is for the outside world to have a positive image of Garfield. We had a chance to show a positive face in 1983 when then presidential candidate John Glenn had a press conference in our auditorium before a live audience of more than fourteen hundred Garfield students. The conference was attended by journalists from the *LA Times*, *La Opinion*, the *East Side Journal*, the local Spanish language television station, and a local English language television station.

We were still having some student incidents at that time, and some of my fellow administrators warned me that I was risking creating some very negative publicity. There were rumors that some students were planning to raise clenched fists during the Pledge of Allegiance and to raise the migrant eagle flag and shout "Chicano Power" while Glenn was speaking.

At that time, we had a lot of special reasons to want to create a positive image of Garfield. I was trying to convince recruiters from major colleges that our school was worth visiting. Some of them were still avoiding us, maybe for fear that their cars would be vandalized, or maybe because they thought Garfield was not producing the kinds of students that their schools wanted. We wanted area universities to send us student teachers and volunteer tutors. We wanted teacher candidates to take us seriously. Escalante had convinced Atlantic Richfield Company (ARCO) to contribute heavily to his math enrichment program, and we were working to get other corporations to follow suit. We could not afford to let a few vocal students mess that up.

I explained to the kids that, while they may have some legitimate grievances, Glenn's press conference was not the place to air them. Garfield was not a nothing school. We were better than that, and we deserved the privilege of this visit and the chance to show our school to the press and to the outside world. Anyone who wanted to bring a complaint to the attention of candidate Glenn could do so in a legitimate way. An orderly, respectful reception would get us further than any rowdy protest. Students with an ax to grind or a statement to make needed to think now of the school, the community, and the common good.

I needed to get a lot of help. I told my student body, "I've got to get your support on this." I had to get the student government involved. I asked teachers to talk to their students and student leaders to address their peers. We could tell that the press was expecting an incident. When the senior class president said, "Let us stand and salute the flag of our nation," every camera swung away from her and toward the students in the audience. Any journalist looking for a sign of disrespect was disappointed. As the students stood politely and began to say the Pledge, the cameras turned slowly back to the stage.

WINNING STUDENT SUPPORT ON MINOR ISSUES

Most of the kids generally supported me on the major issues. The mainstream kids did not identify with the dopers, the gangsters, and the big-time troublemakers. With tardies and skipping, it was different. It was not just the *cholos* and the *vatos locos* who were skipping class and coming in late. When I started cracking down on poor attendance, I got more resistance.

Obviously, the consequence for being tardy was much milder than that for dealing drugs, but a rule is a rule. When we caught cheerleaders, members of the student government, or AP or honor students in a tardy sweep, they thought that they should receive special treatment. The more cooperative kids wanted special treatment because so many kids had more severe infractions, but we had to apply the rules uniformly.

We did not start with the tardy sweeps right away. We waited until we had controlled some of the worst problems first. After mainstream kids saw the positive changes in their restrooms, cafeteria, and hallways, they were more willing to live by rules that directly applied to them. In the spring of

1982 a member of a state accreditation team asked a Garfield senior if I was treading on student rights. He remembered when Garfield had been a much rougher place. He replied, "I don't particularly like Gradillas, but, if he can clean up the gangs and the drugs, I'll gladly give up a few of my rights."

PLAYING THE RACE CARD IN A POSITIVE WAY

In 1968 there had been a big student walkout in East LA. Kids were asking for a better education and Chicano activists had made specific demands. They wanted more Hispanic teachers and administrators, courses in Chicano literature, and more emphasis on Latinos in the history classes. Many of those demands had been met. Our staff was about 40 percent Hispanic, Garfield had a Hispanic principal, we offered Chicano literature, and Hispanics got greater mention in the history classes.

I told the kids that they were receiving what their older brothers and sisters had demanded. I then asked them what they were going to do with what they had won. Did they want Latino pride, or did they want a school with *cholos* fighting, where drug use was prevalent?

LITTLE THINGS MEAN A LOT

When the kids had legitimate complaints or reasonable requests, we tried to do all we could to address them. When kids complained about the food in the cafeteria, we made some changes. First, we added a salad bar, and we offered more and better condiments. When kids asked that Mexican food be served, we added some to the menu. As with the right to have clean restrooms, we felt that the kids had a right to the best food that we could serve them.

When they wanted a nicer prom, we were able to arrange to have one at the Biltmore Hotel. Another year we had the prom at the Sheridan near Universal Studios. The kids, however, understood that there were strings attached. If we were going to make that kind of investment and commitment, we could not have drinking, fighting, or vandalism, and I asked for their help in making sure that there would be none.

I asked teachers to do all they could to recognize and reward accomplishment and positive behavior. I asked them to give certificates of accomplishment when kids did something well. I also asked them to send me names of worthy students, so I could send congratulatory letters home. In 1985 there was an incident off-campus in which a Garfield student was killed. Some of us wore black armbands as a sign of mourning. Kids like it when they know the way that teachers and administrators empathize with them.

We could not get the kids' total support all at once. When we first came in, the kids were a little skeptical. As with the teachers, administrators have to do for the kids before making great demands on them. When we made some changes, most of the kids came to understand that what we were doing was for the common good. Clean bathrooms helped. So did having an orderly cafeteria and safer halls. Support and cooperation from the students increased slowly and steadily for the first three years, and then it peaked and remained high.

During the first year, a lot of the kids, especially the seniors, were used to the old way of doing things. The kids that were coming in from the junior high schools came in as new-order Garfieldians. After three years had passed, all of our kids except the transfers had come through our process. By then, the great majority of our kids liked being Garfieldians.

Chapter Twelve

Involving the Parents

At Garfield we always had a lot of support with parent volunteers when we needed them. Whenever we called for volunteers to help out at sports events or field trips, we got a great turnout. On graduation night, the seniors took buses to Disneyland. We had twelve buses carrying about six hundred kids, and we needed chaperones for all of them. There was never a shortage of parents willing to help.

Every year before the Garfield-Roosevelt game, known as the East Los Angles Classic, there had always been acts of vandalism at both schools. Several parents risked personal injury by patrolling the Garfield grounds the day before the game. When I saw that sort of community spirit, I realized that there was incredible potential for parental support in other areas, including academics.

GETTING PARENT SUPPORT FOR TEACHERS

Teachers depend on parents, but they also sometimes find them troublesome.

In dealing with student discipline, parents are the teachers' first line of defense. When there was a minor problem in the classroom that the teacher was not able to work out directly with the student, I expected the teacher to contact the parents. In most cases, this was enough to resolve the problem. When teachers passed discipline problems on to counselors or administrators, I expected them to send reports of actions they had already taken, including parent contacts.

Teachers find that parents are either their best ally or their biggest problem. If parents understand what their teachers are trying to accomplish, parental rapport is more likely to be positive. Parents react to what the kids tell them, and they're going to hear tales of classroom conflicts told from their children's point of view. If parents ask to initiate a meeting, first with a teacher and later with the principal, they are bound to be angry. If the teacher first contacts the parent and explains the situation, relations will likely be better.

GETTING RELUCTANT PARENTS INTO THE OFFICE

When problems went beyond what the teachers could handle on their own, when kids were chronically truant, or when kids were failing several of their classes, we wanted to see the parents in the office. Sometimes we got the kids to bring their parents in. When kids were performing poorly in their classes, we would remind them that they were in danger of losing their electives or their rights to participate in activities, and often that threat was enough to get their cooperation.

Many families in East LA did not have phones, so communication by mail was especially important. When we sent letters asking parents to speak with us about discipline matters, sometimes students would intercept them and throw them away. We stopped sending bad news in envelopes with the Garfield High School return address. We were given some printed envelopes that bore the names and addresses of area businesses, and sometimes we sent our bad news in those stealth envelopes.

The law did not allow us to keep kids out of school unless they had been suspended or expelled. After a suspension, we could require that the student return with a parent in order to be readmitted to classes. I did not like suspensions because they kept kids out of the place they most needed to be, the classroom. However we were able to use the suspensions as a lever to get the parents to come to the office where we could talk with them. I would often suspend a student at 3:00 p.m., just as school ended, and allow him or her to be reinstated at 8:00 the next morning after meeting with the parents. That way the student would miss little or no class time, but we could force the parents to visit us without violating the letter of the law.

SCHEDULING MEETINGS WITH PARENTS

Many educators think that schools have no responsibility to schedule discipline-related meetings at the parents' convenience. I could not disagree more. We found that we had more parents showing up and we built more good will when we were willing to work around the students' parents' schedules. We were well aware that many of our students' parents could ill afford to take time off of work to meet with us. When someone is raising a family on minimum wage, it is a hardship to lose even one day's pay, so we were willing to schedule meetings before or after school or even on Saturdays. I was always at school by 6:45, so I could usually meet parents before they went to work. If a parent could only come by at 8:00 in the evening, either I stayed around or I made sure that an assistant principal or a counselor was available.

When parents came in to visit me, other people in my office communicated with the parents as well. Sometimes counselors would have issues they wanted to address, and sometimes the school nurse needed to talk with them. Maybe a kid needed glasses or a hearing check, or maybe he or she had been using clinic passes as an excuse to cut class. Sometimes parents were aware of the problems we wanted to discuss, but lot of times the parents had been in the dark. It was not uncommon for us to have attendance problems that the parents did not know anything about until we met with them.

EDUCATING THE PARENTS ABOUT EDUCATION

At Garfield it was especially important to educate the parents about both the value and the demands of a good education. All of our students' parents wanted better lives for their children. They wanted them to have a higher standard of living without the hard physical work many of them did, but many did not understand what their kids had to do in order to attain that. Only a minority of Garfield parents had even a high school education, and some had attended only a few years of elementary school. A few had never been to school at all.

In addition, because of their economic situations, many of our parents relied more heavily on their teenage children than do parents in more affluent communities. They depended on their kids to babysit, to run errands, or to help in family businesses. While we did not try to absolve our students of family responsibilities, we needed the parents to understand that their kids had to attend school regularly and they needed time to study and do homework. I had to explain the demands of the tough academic classes that our students were taking and convince the parents to make accommodations that would allow the children to succeed.

In *Stand and Deliver* Escalante went into a restaurant to talk to the father of one of his students to convince him to let the student stay in school. The real situation was only a little different from the scene depicted in the film. The father of the real student had not ordered his daughter to drop out of school, but she was floundering in calculus class because she had to spend so much of her after-school time supervising waitresses in the family business.

After the conversation with Escalante, the father cut back his daughter's working hours and bought her a study desk for her to use in the restaurant. Situations like this were very common at Garfield.

A lot of our Garfield truants had their parents' permission to skip school. We had to call parents of truants to the office and tell them to not take their kids on extended vacations during the school year, to not take them to their job sites during the school week, to not keep them out of school on holy days of obligation, and to allow them enough freedom from babysitting duties and household chores so that they could attend school every day.

We had a licensed vocational nursing program for fifteen girls at Garfield. Kids in that program spent part of the day taking classes at Garfield and part working in hospitals. Those who completed the course and could pass the state licensed vocational nurse (LVN) exam were licensed to practice nursing upon graduation from high school. We were proud that Garfield was one of only three schools in LAUSD selected to participate in this program. Before my first year at Garfield, on average 60 percent of the kids in the LVN program passed the state test each year. Many of those failures were due to poor attendance.

Beginning in 1982 I allowed students to enter that program only after I met with the parents face-to-face and explained what was expected of them and their children. Both the students and their parents signed contracts in which they agreed that the students would attend classes regularly and do all required class work and homework. In 1984, 90 percent of the students in that program passed the state test.

GARNERING PARENTAL SUPPORT FOR CURRICULAR CHANGE

Convincing the parents of the need for curricular change was key to turning Garfield around. As one might imagine, when we started denying kids their favorite classes in order to make room in their schedules for both academic and remedial classes, there were a lot of parental complaints. At one point, Garfield administrators were talking to an average of four hundred parents per week. Our parent advisory committee meetings grew so large that we had to meet in the auditorium.

Selling our program to the parents was the toughest job I had at Garfield. When I met with the parents I brought in charts and showed them that Garfield High School was at the nineteenth percentile. I compared Garfield's test scores to those of other schools in the district, to its sister schools, and to other schools in the barrio that also have a high number of low-income Hispanics. I also compared Garfield to schools in other states and to the more affluent schools in our district, some of which were posting average scores

THE LAST RESORT

Administrators have the duty to do everything possible to improve the teacher's performance. Some principals have the idea that weak teachers will never improve, and the best policy is to move them out. I have not found this to be the case. About half of the teachers that we targeted for improvement came through for us. Sometimes, however, a teacher will not make the grade, despite the best efforts of the principal and the department head.

In such cases, the principal needs to start a paper trail to use as evidence that serious attempts were made to rehabilitate the teacher. An arbitrator or a judge is going to ask, "What assistance did you give this teacher once you determined that he was below standard?" The administration must be prepared to produce a log that shows the time that administrators and the department head worked to help the teacher improve. When administrators can establish that they had bent over backwards to help the teacher improve, the judge or hearing officer will almost certainly rule in their favor.

around the 90th percentile. I mailed home the CTBS scores of each individual kid and circled in red what the scores were and what they should be.

After I started making an issue of Garfield's failings, there was a lot of tension as everyone began playing the blame game. When a patient comes out of a fifty-five year coma, there is going to be some discomfort. The first suggestion from the parents was to fire the teachers. Of course, the teachers placed a big part of the blame on the parents. I had to handle these responses delicately to avoid a backlash. I needed the teachers and the parents to be partners, not adversaries.

After we started making changes in rules and curriculum, a lot of parents were unhappy with the stricter rules and the greater work requirements. After we got a positive school climate in place, parental support grew by leaps and bounds. The reduced gang activity, the lack of graffiti, the increasingly less-frequent visits from the police were noticed and appreciated. When Garfield kids started going to Ivy League colleges on full scholarships, the community really took notice.

TAPPING THE ORGANIZATIONS

We had a lot of parents of Garfield kids who were very involved in school organizations. We had a large booster club that supported our athletic teams, and a large band booster club that raised money to pay for uniforms and fund band trips. We also had a large PTA. In all, the membership of the various parent organizations at Garfield represented the parents of about half the kids at our school.

At first, the booster clubs pretty much stuck to sports and music, and the PTA was mostly a social organization. The PTA raised funds for activities and made coffee and baked cookies to serve at open houses and other after-school functions. While I appreciated what they were doing, I also wanted their help in building school climate and improving the curriculum. Several members of these organizations at first expressed that those responsibilities were mine.

I needed strong parental support for the changes that we were making at Garfield. We could not have mandated Saturday classes for academically weak students if the parents did not support us by getting their kids out of bed and sending them to school on Saturday mornings. We could not have made algebra a graduation requirement or knocked kids out of sports or electives in order to give them remedial reading and math unless a large number of parents understood our reasons and approved.

Before we started cracking down on drugs and fights, we had to let the parents know that these things would not be tolerated, and, on a few occasions, kids would be led out of school in handcuffs. We did not want this to be a surprise, and we wanted the parents to know why we were taking these steps.

I needed to reach large numbers of parents, and I did so by meeting them where they gathered. During my first few years as principal at Garfield, there was rarely an after-school meeting of a parent group that I did not attend, or at least drop in on for a few minutes. Before we started changing Garfield's curriculum, I wanted the parents to understand there would be some hardships.

We explained to the booster clubs that a new, tougher curriculum would cause some kids to be dropped from sports and the band until they got their skills and grades up, but that these changes were worth the pain. We explained to the PTA the importance of an improved school climate and the steps we had to take to create one. We asked the leaders of these groups to canvas their members and tell me what the parents wanted. We also asked them to help us spread our message to as many Garfield parents as possible.

When we first put the algebra requirement in place, there were the predictable parental complaints to the superintendent. When major changes are made at a school, the main office is going to get more calls from discontented squeaky wheels than from parents who are happy about the new way of doing things. The minutes from the meetings of the various school organizations provided proof that we did have substantial parental support for what we were doing. It is hard for a superintendent whose complaint is based on a few phone calls to refute minutes and letters indicating support from every major parent group on campus.

Some PTA members never deviated from their former roles. They still made coffee and cookies, and they still provided volunteer help when we needed greeters and chaperones. I am glad that they did, but we also got PTA support in academic and school climate matters. Our GT parents advisory group actively supported our academic decathlon team by raising money for T-shirts and study materials, chaperoning field trips for participants, and sponsoring events to honor participants and winners. Other parent groups began to lend their support as well.

We eventually added several other booster clubs, this time academic boosters. We had a parent group for the computer/science magnet program. We had another for our AP program. These parents raised money to help defray the costs of the AP exams. I was delighted when these groups and the PTA started working together. Instead of being special interest groups working in isolation, our parent groups came together to work for the good of all students.

Chapter Thirteen

Other Support Groups

Sometimes administrators are afraid of having community members in the school and teachers are afraid to have community members in their classrooms. Usually these fears are ungrounded. The more the community feels that their school is an open book, the more likely they are to cooperate with educators.

In the military I learned that it's never a good idea to go it alone. The most successful infantry operations were carried out with air and artillery support. Even Escalante could not have succeeded without a lot of outside support. There is a lot of support to be found in the community. Small, local businesses, Fortune 500 companies, postsecondary education organizations, social services, and political groups can all provide a lot of assistance to schools and do much to enhance the quality of kids' education. Partnering with these elements instead of acting as adversaries will only cause schools to improve.

GETTING HELP FROM BUSINESSES

Local small business in a school's attendance zone, from the nearby taco stands and gas stations to manufacturing concerns, can provide advice, speakers, services, and financial support. Fortune 500 companies, including those that do not have operations in a school's attendance zone, can provide contributions for scholarships, equipment, and supplies. They can also provide speakers and advisors. Often businesses are the first to complain about the quality of an area school's graduates. When businesses express concerns, schools have an opening to get these businesses involved.

A lot of our kids at Garfield were working part-time jobs, and sometimes these jobs got in the way of their schoolwork. I asked people in the community to only give Garfield kids jobs if they were attending school regularly and maintaining acceptable grades. California requires that schools sign a work permit for students under the age of eighteen. At one time, those permits were rubber stamped. I instituted a policy of only signing if both attendance and grades were good.

That was only reasonable. If the local business community expected us to send them graduates who were well prepared for careers in their enterprises, it was reasonable for us to ask that they help us motivate kids to attend regularly and maintain good grades. After all, if business people were letting failing Garfield students stay up late at night doing poorly paid menial work when they should be doing school work, they had no right to complain that our graduates did not have the skills their businesses wanted.

We had a full-time work experience coordinator on campus. One of the tasks I assigned him was to visit businesses that employed Garfield kids without getting or maintaining work permits. He would tell employers that they would either have to follow the procedure or else we would report them to the Board of Labor for violation of child labor laws. Our center also served as an employment agency for our kids. Employers could come to Garfield and find students who were available for part-time employment. As time went by and Garfield's reputation improved, many area employers sought out Garfield students.

We liked to have local businesspeople and professionals talk to our kids on career night. While we invited speakers of all races, we especially liked to have minorities talk to our kids about careers, because too many of our kids thought that career success was for Whites and Asians, and that they were locked out of the world of the middle class. Seeing successful professionals who were local people who looked like them, who grew up in their neighborhoods, and who knew the same people they knew helped convince many that success was not something just for other people.

Businesses gave us a lot of financial support. In the 1985–1986 school year, different Garfield programs received over $300,000 in contributions from various businesses. ARCO contributed $100,000 to Escalante's math enrichment program. Escalante personally solicited the first contributions for his program. ARCO was so impressed with Escalante's program and its results that it continued making contributions for several years. MIT professor and electronics entrepreneur Amar Bose was so impressed with the former Garfield students that he encountered in his classes that he came to Garfield to meet Escalante. He personally contributed $10,000 in electronic equipment to Escalante and helped arrange MIT scholarships for Escalante students.

Sometimes the LA Lakers gave Escalante free tickets so he could offer to take the students who scored highest on a test to a dinner and a game. Corporate donations also paid for prizes like free dinners. Steak and lobster in a Beverly Hills restaurant along with a reminder that such meals are within the reach of engineers and other professionals can be quite an eye-opener for a kid who has only been out of the East LA barrio a few times.

During the 1984 Los Angeles Olympics the Australian women's basketball team used Garfield's gym to practice and train. This gave us the opportunity to approach Coca-Cola, an Olympic sponsor. Coke expressed interest in helping us with a dropout prevention program. I had a written plan for an as yet unfunded program for kids who had consistently had poor attendance in middle school and who seemed at risk for dropping out of Garfield. We had been hoping to fund a school within a school for these kids.

Coke offered us $50,000 per year. We accepted their offer and established our new program. We paid the teachers from regular school funds, but the corporate contribution allowed us to offer a lot of field trips and to hire a special full-time counselor just for that program. That program was a tremendous success. By the end of its third year, the absentee rate among these students was actually lower than that of the rest of the school.

When we set up a computer magnet school, we bought all of the computers for that program from IBM. After the IBM rep saw the pathetic collection of antique manual and electric typewriters in our business classes, he arranged for his company to donate thirty-two state-of-the-art electric typewriters to our business program. Later IBM gave us an entire computer lab, including work stations and software.

When we were paring down Garfield's vocational offerings, a representative from the Ford Motor Company expressed concern about the future of our auto shop program. I told him that I really wanted to keep auto shop alive, but only if it could be state of the art. The Ford Company responded by giving us a brand new car for our auto shop kids to work on as well as some computer diagnostic equipment.

Local small businesses helped out financially as well. I visited businesses myself, or I sent assistant principals, counselors, or teachers to ask for contributions. I usually had a few Garfield students come along with us. We got turned down a lot, but sometimes we got what we asked for, and sometimes we came away with something that was not what we were asking for but still was useful.

One bank manager told me that his bank did not make direct contributions for school operations, but it was willing to contribute to scholarship funds. One bank gave us $500 toward the purchase of textbooks. Another paid for a banquet to honor some of our AP students. A local pizza restaurant paid to print the tickets for all of our athletic events. Sometimes they would print on the ticket a coupon for a discount on one of their products, so we both benefited. Local car dealerships loaned us cars for homecoming festivities. Various businesses contributed toward the purchase of plaques, trophies, and other awards.

There are two special advantages to funding educational programs with private contributions. These private contributions tell students that the outside world recognizes their accomplishments. Since private donors expect results for their largess, this also gives students yet another reason to endeavor to excel. They learn quickly that continued support from the private sector must be earned.

EDUCATIONAL ORGANIZATIONS

We liked to get representatives from colleges around Garfield as much as possible. Not only did very few kids at Garfield have parents who had graduated from college, many did not even have any college-educated acquaintances. A lot of these kids were pretty bright, but higher education was a mystery to them. We had the college nights like every other high school in the country, but we went one step further. One office in the counseling section was designated the college corner. We had a full-time counselor whose only job was to give kids advice and assistance related to selecting and applying to colleges and universities.

We invited representatives of institutions of higher learning to visit us as often as possible. Often these reps would speak in a class or two and then spend the rest of the day in the college corner talking to kids on a one-to-one basis. I got to be a pretty good friend of Dr. David Pierpont Gardner, the president of the University of California system, and sometimes he would come down personally and talk to our kids. Some of our kids had really done their college application homework. Gardner was impressed when he found Garfield kids weighing the relative merits of UCLA, USC, UC Santa Barbara, and Berkley.

USC and UCLA were within a short driving distance, but in many ways they were light years away from many of our kids. I wanted our kids to be around the representatives of academia, talk to them, and become comfortable with them so that they could see that universities were places that they could fit into. College reps also spoke to our teachers and administrators, both in faculty meetings and in inservices, explaining what they expected of their entering freshmen and what we at Garfield could do to better prepare our kids to succeed in their institutions.

At one time a lot of nineteen- and twenty-year-old Garfield graduates would come back and hang around the hallways. After we tightened up security they were not able to get into school to loiter, but we did welcome

Garfield alums to come on campus through proper channels and talk to current students. We especially welcomed former students who were attending academic powerhouses like Cal Tech, MIT, Stanford, and the Ivies. Sometimes these alums would be friends of kids who were still in Garfield, so they were excellent peer role models. These peer talks were real eye-openers. To some of our kids it was news that a college class might only have one or two graded tests and a single research paper in a semester.

East Los Angeles College (ELAC) provided facilities for Escalante's summer program, which provided and still provides math classes for students from all over East Los Angeles. Escalante started giving summer math classes to Garfield kids, and eventually expanded the program to include kids from other area high schools as well. We found that the ELAC administration was easier to deal with than our own LAUSD central office.

I was chastised by my superiors for accepting ARCO's $100,000 donation for Escalante's math program, and I was told that the following year we would have to turn the money over to the district, which would then mete it out at its discretion. Of course, that would have been the end of the grant. ARCO chose to donate to Escalante's program because of their faith that there would be solid results there. They did not want to donate to a general fund for the district. We suggested to ARCO that they give the money to ELAC, where it was spent in Escalante's summer program.

We eventually set up a program on the ELAC campus where students could take required high school classes from Garfield teachers and then take electives from ELAC teachers. Three LAUSD schools, Monroe, University High, and Birmingham, had universities nearby and programs that allowed their students to take some of their classes on those university campuses, and we wanted the same opportunities for our kids. Garfield was having a space problem then. Our student population was growing, but our building was not. We had to move several bungalows onto campus in order to accommodate all of our students.

ELAC was not so crowded, so there were facilities there to accommodate several of our kids. One problem that we had was that ELAC, though near, was not within walking distance of Garfield. California law required kids enrolled in regular high school to attend four high school classes per day in order to be considered present. They could take college classes beyond those four, but four had to be taught by teachers certified to teach secondary school. We solved that problem by housing several of our Garfield teachers on the ELAC campus. The first year this program was made available to juniors, who were then allowed to attend the following year as well.

Our kids took their four core classes from those teachers in the morning and then they were free to take electives and other academic classes offered by ELAC in the afternoon. Those classes counted for high school credit, but they appeared on an ELAC transcript and were valid if the students continued at ELAC or transferred to colleges that would accept ELAC credit. These kids had ELAC library cards and access to most ELAC facilities, and they were eligible to participate in many ELAC activities.

This program offered a college opportunity for our academically second-tier kids. The kids who were taking three or four AP classes per term were not interested. Those students were not planning to attend community college. They were bound for the Ivies, Stanford, MIT, or UC.

SOCIAL SERVICES

We had two major challenges with social services. One was to convince marginalized kids that social service providers, especially the police, were to work for them, not against them. The other challenge was that some of the social services worked mostly with the parents, and we wanted them to also work more closely with the kids.

A lot of demands are made on schools, demands that many educators feel are unreasonable. In addition to providing an academic education, schools are expected to provide food, transportation, moral guidance, counseling, sex and drug education, and even a level of health care, including mental health services. Schools like Garfield were asked to provide even more than the average American school because of the limited financial resources of most of the parents in the community. An African proverb says that it takes a village to raise a child. It takes an array of social services to provide all that is asked of modern schools.

Garfield had one full-time nurse, one half-time nurse, and an LAUSD physician who was on campus two or three days per month. A lot of our parents lacked health insurance. Many of our students were recent immigrants who either had not had the immunizations that California law required in order for them to enroll in school, or else the immunization records were missing. Many of our students were in need of preventive procedures that would allow them to remain healthy. Obviously, our clinic staff could not handle a task that big alone. We worked closely with a number of clinics and public hospitals in the area to match kids in need with available health-related services.

In chapter 4, I discussed our policy on drug use. We had zero tolerance for drug possession and use on campus, but we were as concerned about preventing drug use as we were about removing those who brought drugs to our campus. We asked area hospitals, clinics, and health services to send us drug educators to talk to our kids both in their classes and in counseling sessions. We also brought in reformed former drug abusers to tell kids how difficult their habits had made their lives. We had to screen the latter group carefully, since we found that a few were not as reformed as they claimed to be, and some spoke with thinly veiled nostalgia for their former lives.

We had ten counselors and a part-time psychologist at Garfield, but a great many mental-health services were also available through area clinics and hospitals and through county agencies. Our counselors often made referrals to them. We had both district and county social workers available to us. Educators are required to report suspected child abuse to Child Protective Services, and, of course, I expected my staff to do so, but we also called on these social workers to help out with other problems as well. While there are no rules that prevent educators from visiting our students' parents' homes, most have little time to do so. In many cases, it is easier for social workers to make home visits.

LAW ENFORCEMENT AGENCIES

Like everyone else, we relied on the fire and police departments for protection. We welcomed the fire department's inspections. In fact, I asked fire inspectors to come in and inspect more often than was required. With all the electrical gadgets in modern classrooms, there are a lot of potential fire hazards, and it is important to keep teachers aware of safety procedures.

A lot of our kids felt that they and the police were on opposite sides. We had two programs geared to help the kids understand law enforcement. One was *Teacher and the Law* and the other was *Student and the Law*. The former brought police officers into faculty meetings and inservices to train our teachers about laws that affect their jobs. The latter was directed at the kids. At first, that program involved mostly the gang kids. Later we expanded it. We brought peace officers and fire fighters into school and had them talk to our social studies classes.

We stressed to the kids the importance of treating the police with respect. If someone is stopped by a peace officer on Whittier Boulevard at two in the morning it can be dangerous to behave in a threatening manner. I told the kids that, if they were really treated in a truly inappropriate manner by a police officer or other authority figure, to report the situation to me, and I would investigate, but, if the accusation was false, the accuser would pay a price. We must have got our message across. In 1985 the sheriff told me that he and other officers in his department found Garfield kids to be the best behaved group in East LA.

GOVERNMENT BODIES AND POLITICAL ORGANIZATIONS

As with the government agencies, a lot of our kids did not feel that government law-making bodies worked for them, and they did not understand how they could themselves participate and make those bodies work for them. Inner-city neighborhoods are well known for protests, sit-ins, and walkouts. The 1968 East LA walkout is even chronicled in some history books. When I first came to Garfield a lot of Chicano advocacy groups from the area, like the Mexican-American Commission, Cleland House, MECHA (a Spanish acronym for Chicano Student Movement of Aztlan), and *Si Se Puede* (Spanish for Yes We Can), were pretty active on campus.

Representatives of these groups came to see me often, and we were often at odds. I agreed with these groups about many of their goals. Their hearts may have been in the right place, but many of their actions were counterproductive. Usually when they came to see me it was to challenge a suspension, transfer, or arrest, or to protest changes that raised academic standards. Sometimes these groups encouraged kids to change things by making noise.

A lot of representatives of these groups liked to talk to our kids in the hallways or in the cafeteria. When we started to control access to our campus and we required visitors to go through appropriate channels, they came less and less. Their popularity waned among our students as time went by and our students began to learn how to use other channels to make themselves heard.

I wanted our students to understand that sit-ins, strikes, and vocal protests are not the most effective ways to get things done. Escalante's kids did not get full scholarships to America's top colleges by marching and shouting. I wanted the kids to understand the means to use the system to really effect change: how to petition, how to negotiate, and how to get one's voice heard by and through public officials.

We liked to get school board members, local councilmen, and state reps into our classrooms as much as possible. We wanted our kids to understand the concept of representative government and to know that their representatives could and should be approached. I asked my government teachers to bring local politicians to speak to their classes whenever possible. School board member and later city councilwoman Gloria Molina and California Senator Art Torres visited and spoke on a regular basis. We even hosted a press conference for a presidential candidate, John Glenn.

Sometimes parents of failing, suspended, or transferred kids would contact school board members or local councilmen and ask them to talk to me. I would always receive them and hear their complaints, although I rarely acted on them, but I would ask, "Since you're going to be on campus, would you mind addressing Mrs. _____'s government class?"

Chapter Fourteen

Dealing with Other Powers That Be

Again, the position of a principal is much like that of the captain of a ship. The principal is the supreme authority in the school, just as the captain is on a ship. Still, the principal is not a dictator and certainly should not try to act as one. There are other forces and authorities both inside and outside of the school, and a principal needs to be able to work with all of them.

DEALING WITH THE UPPER ADMINISTRATION

I found it really hilarious when the principals that I mentioned in chapter 2 told me that my superiors did not bother me the way their superiors bothered them. I was once told by a district administrator that his office had to deal with more complaints, requests, concerns, and grievances from Garfield than any other fifteen high schools combined.

To many district administrators, Escalante and I, along with a growing group of like-minded teachers and administrators, were becoming a huge source of irritation and frustration. Still, the district guidelines stated that all district staff and offices existed to support principals and staffs of the schools, K–12. I expected and demanded that support, and, for the most part, I got it.

When I began at Garfield, LAUSD was divided into eight areas. Each area had its own superintendent, curriculums specialists, and personnel office. At the top of the pyramid was the central office, known to LAUSD employees as Downtown or the Hill. Garfield was one of six high schools in area G. My second year, all forty-nine regular high schools in LAUSD were taken from the direct control of the area administrations and turned over to the newly formed high school division.

I was fortunate in several ways when I began at Garfield. I had worked at Garfield as a teacher and later as the dean of discipline four years before, so I was familiar with the school, the community, and many of the employees. I did begin with sort of a mandate. Some teachers, including Jaime Escalante and Ralph Heiland, Garfield's union rep, had petitioned the central office to get me transferred there.

When the high school district was formed after my first year at the Garfield helm, Paul Possemato, who had been my principal when I was dean of discipline at Garfield, was named its superintendent. He understood both the situation at Garfield and my way of doing things, and we both respected one another, so I had a good working relationship with my immediate supervisor.

One problem with the creation of the high school district was that it gave me a third set of superiors. Although I no longer answered directly to the area G administration, I was housed in that area, and the schools that fed Garfield were under its direct control, so we felt their impact and influence at Garfield as well. Shortly after I took over, I upset a lot of people in higher administration. I started making demands that they were not prepared for. I also generated a lot of complaints when I increased the number of suspensions, expulsions, and transfers.

I started demanding things that more affluent schools took for granted. I wanted more and better books, better-qualified teachers, and money for field trips to places like art museums. It was not racism or any malevolent thinking that caused Garfield to be denied these things. It was just that Garfield had never asked for them before, so we had to fight inertia. Garfield was supposed to be a low-performing school, so any extra funding that we got was supposed to be spent on remedial or vocational instruction. That is the way it had been in the past.

We were also expected to accept problems that were not tolerated at more affluent schools. It was accepted Downtown that Latino kids would fight, that the gangs would always be around the barrio and in the barrio schools, and that attendance in schools like Garfield would always be poor. No one expected me to turn a completely blind eye to drug use, but some of the higher-ups were uncomfortable with my turning drug dealers and users over to the police.

I had to really stand firm on that one. Drugs are drugs, whether they are consumed in East LA or the San Fernando Valley. If a school becomes the only public place in the neighborhood where drug dealers and users do not have to fear the law, then school becomes the safest place in the neighborhood to use and deal drugs. It was not fair to our serious students to allow drug users and dealers to act with impunity on our campus. In a way, we were ahead of our time. We set policies designed to make Garfield a drug- and weapon-free zone years before the federal Safe Schools mandate.

DEALING WITH PARENTS' COMPLAINTS TO UPPER ADMINISTRATION

All three administrative offices fielded complaints from parents. My first year, both the area G office and Downtown passed a lot of those complaints on to me. I told them that I had to do some house cleaning. There were no gang *placas* scrawled on the walls of Beverly Hills High School, and kids there did not have to compete for space with pot smokers when they needed to use the restroom. Garfield kids deserved the same.

As time went by, the number of complaints dropped. As people in the community saw that we could take the schools back from the gangs, support for what we were doing increased.

Before that time, it took some politicking to keep my superiors at bay. If the parent of a student whom I had suspended for assaulting another student complained to the area superintendent, I suggested that parents of the victim speak up as well. Garfield was not full of happy campers then, so I asked that my superiors not judge me by my first year. An athlete is not judged by the first leg of the race, but by the final time.

In 1986 the office of the superintendent of the high school division formally recognized Garfield as the high school with the least number of expulsions, suspensions, and police interventions among all forty-nine high schools in the district. I was invited to address a group of administrators to explain the reasons for our success. When the superintendent asked how we did it, I asked him in turn, "Don't you remember what we did a few years ago to establish the school climate?"

GREASING THE SQUEAKIEST WHEELS

Our no-fighting rule was tested to the limit when two senior girls, one an honor student and the other an outstanding athlete, got into a physical altercation at a football game. Both girls were suspended and sent to another LAUSD school on an opportunity transfer.

Shortly thereafter I started getting telephone calls from both the district office and the election committee for a California state senator. The parents of one of the girls were pressuring both the district and the senator to get their daughter reinstated. The district office was pretty insistent. This put me in a real bind. It had taken an entire year to get to the point where we could ban fighting at Garfield. Reinstating the young lady could take us back to square one. If an honor student with political connections could fight on our campus and not suffer the consequences, belligerents from opposing gangs would demand equally lenient treatment.

I had to cut a deal on this one. I contacted the parents and asked if there was anything that we could do short of reinstating their daughter that would satisfy them. They answered that they wanted their daughter to receive a Garfield diploma and to graduate on our stage with her Garfield classmates. The first condition was a non-issue, since we had already decided that both girls would receive Garfield diplomas. That was only fair since they had received all but a few months of their education with us. I immediately agreed to the second condition, the wheel got enough grease to stop the squeak, and the integrity of our no-fighting rule was maintained.

DEALING WITH BUREAUCRATIC RESISTANCE TO RAISING ACADEMIC STANDARDS

After Garfield's climate was under control, we still had a long way to go. Most of our kids came to us several years behind academically. If they were to catch up to grade level, many of them would have to advance two grade levels in each year they spent with us, and that took money. The central office got sick of me asking for more money, books, teachers, equipment, and so forth. A lot of our parents and teachers, among them Escalante, were making more demands than the people upstairs were used to fielding from our corner of the district.

The job of an upper-level administrator is a bit like that of someone watching a panel with a few hundred warning lights on it. When one light is flashing all the time, that makes the monitor uncomfortable. A lot of my superiors wanted me to stop making waves. One told me, "You've cleaned up the gangs, the walls are painted, and you've got flowers planted around the building. You've won the respect of the parents and the administration. Why don't you rest on your laurels and enjoy life?" That was not the time to rest. After a patient comes out of a coma, the doctors and nurses do not just congratulate themselves and go out for coffee. The patient needs to get out of bed, and there must be physical therapy so that the patient's physical and mental condition can be restored.

THE BUDGET

The most important job of the higher-level administration is to allocate and monitor the funds that we principals use to operate our schools. After the first few years, getting the money we needed was not a great problem. After Garfield's reputation improved and we were able to show the area and main offices that our kids were benefiting from museum field trips and AP offerings, it became easier to get them to cooperate in funding matters. Still, funding is finite and, if a school takes only that which is freely given by the school district, it will come up short.

The regular funding will cover the meat and potatoes, but a school has to look beyond the regular budget for the dessert. Also, having outside channels for funding allows a school an extra modicum of freedom and flexibility. If teachers want a special set of books or a certain piece of equipment that the district will not fund, it is nice to have other sources to turn to. This is one reason why it is so important to raise some funds from the private sector.

All educators need to understand that most monies allocated to schools are categorical. GT funds have to pass through GT teachers' hands, ESL funds have to pass through ESL teachers' hands, and so on. Usually there are formulae for allotment: a certain percentage for staff, another for staff development, another for materials, and so forth. It is best for a principal to let go of the reins of categorical funds. Their use is determined before they ever get to the campus. With noncategorical funds and funds that come through grants and private sector donations, there are more choices.

Occasionally programs harm the kids that they are supposed to help. This was the case with American-born, English-dominant kids who were being served in our ESL program. When we kicked these kids out of the nest and made them study language arts in classes that are designed for kids who speak English, we lost money, but the kids gained. It is never a good idea to pretend that students have an academic deficit just to keep money flowing.

Even though an administrator should never lie to get money, sometimes a little creative budgeting, as long as it is within the law and benefits the kids, is worth doing. I once had a situation where we had more students than desks, but there were no monies available to buy new desks. There was, however, money budgeted to replace older, defective desks. We had a lot of junk, including several old, broken desks piled up outside of our custodians' storage building. I took them to the central warehouse where they were replaced with new ones. Sometimes principals can do some horse swapping. One man's trash is another's treasure, and sometimes another school's surplus served to fill some of our teachers' needs.

INVOLVING THE STAFF IN BUDGETARY MATTERS

It is best to get the staff involved in budget decisions. The more involvement there is, the better the staff will understand how funding works. Often the principals are blamed for funding matters over which they have little control. When the staff is involved and understands how budgeting works, teachers who understand funding regulations and limitations will explain the real reasons for funding dilemmas to their peers. If possible, committees that influence budget matters should have input from parents as well.

Teachers should have access to individual material accounts (IMA), and they should, for the most part, be able to spend those funds at their discretion, but those accounts need to be guarded. An inexperienced teacher might wipe out an entire IMA on field trips or textbooks and not have anything left for chalk and paper. Principals need a formula for fund allocations. Some classes cost more to teach than others. Because of equipment requirements, an auto shop class costs more to run than an English class.

WORKING WITH THE UNIONS

The union and the school board have contracts, and administrators need to understand the contracts as well as the union reps do. Most administrators who have problems with the unions either do not know the contract or attempt to circumvent it. I know one principal who violated the contractual requirement that all teachers have a thirty-minute duty-free lunch by requiring each teacher to take lunch duty once per week. He lost that battle. If something is spelled out in black and white, why fight it?

Sometimes the union reps would tell me that I was pushing the envelope, and sometimes I would agree and back off, although sometimes we had to work matters out. Of course, I often stood my ground. Usually, matters of working conditions were pretty clear. Since contracts typically did not deal with matters of instruction, instructional issues could be more contentious.

Unions wanted the same thing that I did: happy teachers. While we did not always agree, for the most part, they worked with me. We once had a conflict over the size of Escalante's classes. The contract specified that no academic class would have over thirty-seven students. Even though Escalante did not want his class size reduced, I could understand the union's concern. If we could put forty-five kids in every class, teachers would be laid off.

Escalante's circumstances were unlike those of other teachers in the district. His calculus class had become wildly popular. If I reduced his class size, we would either have to drop kids from calculus or else place them with a less able teacher. Besides that, Escalante's situation was unique. He had paid student aides and tutors. We agreed to designate Escalante's class a pilot program and allow him to play by different rules. I agreed that I would hire another calculus teacher if I could find one of Escalante's caliber, and the union agreed to help me look for one.

Sometimes principals get upset with union representatives for doing their job. If a rep defends a teacher who a principal feels is ineffective, the principal should not take offense. Teachers who are in danger of being demoted or losing their positions have the right to state their cases and to have appropriate representation. In these cases, principals need to put on their hats and let the union reps put on theirs.

I found that union reps could be very helpful in getting mentoring help for marginal teachers. It is the union's job to protect teachers and to keep them working. If I brought it to a local union leader's attention that a certain teacher was in need of help and that he or she would not have his or her contract renewed unless I saw some improvement, union people would usually help us out. This benefited the rank and file, the management, and the students.

EFFECTIVELY ENACTING SITE-BASED MANAGEMENT

When a new education trend comes into play, administrators can deal with it in one of three ways: They can fight it, ignore it and wait for it to go away, or look at it and prepare for change. When I was at Garfield, site-based management (SBM) was not yet a buzzword. I did, however, involve personnel in important decisions because I needed their input. SBM is a major plus if the staff and the community want it. When I became principal of Birmingham High in 1991, we became one of the first schools in LA to implement site-based management. The former principal had resisted the change.

For the most part, I welcomed the new system, but I wanted control over the budget. After all, ultimately I was the one held responsible. It was not hard to get a sensible level of control of the budget. I told the committees to bring me a budget that I could use. After two months of discussion, the committees could not reach an agreement, so they ended up willingly turning that power over to me.

I also asked to have some authority in hiring and removing staff. Teachers do not want to be responsible for firing their own, so that part was not a problem. As far as hiring, I would choose a pool of four or five qualified applicants and then let committees choose from them. As long as they were all good candidates, it did not much matter to me which one was chosen.

There must be trust if SBM is to work. I contested the committee's hiring decisions only twice in four and a half years. I did so because I had confidential information about the applicants that I could not legally share with the staff. By that time, the staff trusted me enough to accept my decisions.

Principals who are angry with site-based management do not understand it. Often principals can use SBM to their advantage. Over the years I had managed to step on a few LAUSD toes, so some of the administrators in the central office had their sights on me. If they attempted to reject one of our proposals at Birmingham, they were not just rejecting me, but rather everyone who had signed. When a superintendent sees six signatures, he treats a proposal differently.

Chapter Fifteen

The Garfield Model, Then and Now

More than two decades have passed since I was principal at Garfield High School. There have been some major changes since then. No Child Left Behind, the Safe Schools Act, the revised IDEA Law, and advances in technology have changed the face of education in many ways. It is no longer heresy to ask inner-city kids to take algebra. In fact, in California algebra is now a requirement for graduation. We have test-driven curricula, more emphasis on academic subjects, and better tools to help schools deal with weapons and drugs. Even elementary schools in the poorest school districts have computers. Still, the more things change, the more they stay the same.

A lot of what was happening in the eighties is still going on. Not enough kids are being challenged to their full potential. Too many kids drop out of high school, or even middle school. A lot of kids are still bailing out of the most difficult classes. When kids perform poorly in school, people still blame race and socioeconomic status. Tracking is still going on, although it is better concealed than it once was.

Twenty and thirty years ago, we had fights and gang violence, but we were not seeing Columbine-type mass murders in our schools. On the bright side, technology has made surveillance equipment affordable, and the attention that high-profile disasters have drawn has helped make school security a priority. I had to struggle with the central office to get the kind of security equipment that is now standard in schools all over the country. People no longer say, "It can't happen here."

While principals have always had the power to enforce rules against drugs and weapons, the Safe Schools law forces the hand of principals who would otherwise go light on drug and weapon offenders. Today nobody questions a school's right to bring in drug sniffing dogs or to search lockers for weapons. When dealing with infractions that are not felonies or gross misdemeanors, however, many schools do no more to promote an orderly environment than they were doing twenty years ago. Kids still want an orderly school climate, and too many schools are still failing to provide one.

THE IMPACT OF STANDARDIZED TESTING

With NCLB-driven monitoring of dropout numbers and test scores, more pressure is on educators to get their students to perform. That should make the Garfield experience more relevant than ever. I did not feel the extreme pressure to improve numbers that today's administrators experience. My problem was the opposite. Downtown told me that high dropout rates and poor test scores went with the territory and that I should accept them. In this age of data-driven education, positive statistics are the Holy Grail. Our top priority was not to produce positive statistics, but rather to give our kids the best education that we could offer them. The higher test scores and lower dropout rates were fortunate by-products of improved education.

For today's schools, many of the dynamics have changed. Today, in part because the law demands that kids pass state tests, often the best instruction is geared to the bubble kids, those who are in danger of failing the test, and the students who are test exempt and those who are certain to pass sometimes get shortchanged.

Too often important content is left untaught because standardized tests do not include it. When the state test does not cover the entire curriculum, sometimes the test is taught, but the entire curriculum is not covered. If the curriculum is fifty feet deep, and the test only covers ten of those feet . . . you get the idea. We have seen a huge increase in kids passing state tests, but we still have a lot of kids who cannot recognize a sonnet or define a classical tragedy.

Then, as now, when teachers were blamed for poor grades, some responded by watering down their courses. A teacher of a watered-down course can claim success if his students score well on a watered-down test. In some states, the same seems to be happening with state assessments. Even though scores on state tests keep rising, SAT and National Assessment of Educational Progress (NAEP) scores are stagnant, and colleges are complaining about the academic skills of the kids the high schools send them. The public needs to question how rigorous some of the state tests really are.

TECHNOLOGY, FOR BETTER AND WORSE

Technology has been a mixed blessing. All students get computer training beginning in elementary school, or even before. Even low-income kids carry around cellular phones that have more computing power than NASA had when they sent the first man into space. Through the Internet, kids have access to entire libraries of information. It is wonderful that kids know how to use this technology. Technology has also been a big plus with school/ parent communication. Schools have websites that post everything from school news to student grades. Parents and teachers can stay in touch with e-mail, and classroom-to-office communications are instantaneous.

Like everything else, good use of technology is a question of balance. There are a lot of abuses. Some kids now text each other and play computer games in class when they should be doing challenging academic work. Cell phones and PDAs are the new crib sheets, and the Internet is making plagiarism as easy as cut and paste. Freshman English instructors are complaining that kids who spent their school years creating multimedia presentations instead of writing research papers don't have the writing skills they need to succeed in college.

I experienced another misuse of technology when I served as a principal in Comstock, Michigan, in 2002–2003. I left LAUSD before everybody started communicating by email, so I was surprised when I saw that I was getting twenty or thirty electronic communications every day on my school computer. The administrators, teachers, and parents who sent them expected quick responses. If I had sent answers when the senders wanted them, I would have had to stay in my office tied to the computer all day. An office-bound principal cannot be an effective principal. It is more important than ever for principals to prioritize. E-mailers need to either be patient in waiting for responses or else deal with someone who has time to stay at a desk.

THE NEW DUMPING GROUNDS

Even though vocational education is no longer the dumping ground it once was, dumping grounds still exist. The worst dumping ground is the pool of dropouts, or pushouts. In some states, a student can legally drop out of school at the age of sixteen with parental permission. In many other states the official age is eighteen, but the *de facto* age is much lower. You do not see truancy officers rounding up high-school kids very often. We even hear stories about kids being encouraged to drop out or transfer to GED programs in order to keep average test scores high. That is really a perverse use of the system.

Alternative schools can help kids who have problems that keep them from succeeding on a regular campus. An older student who has hung around school too long might be better off getting a job and going to night school. A young mother might only be able to go to a school that provides day care. Some students might need either a more structured or a less structured environment than the regular campuses offer. Still, some alternative schools do not offer their students anything extra other than low standards.

Charter schools have been a mixed blessing. Some are excellent, and Escalante and I have wondered if we could have kept his dynasty alive if we had turned Garfield into a charter school back in the eighties. Still, as with the alternative schools, there are charter schools that do not offer much more than lax rules and academic credit for poor performance. It does not matter what we call the classes or the schools. Kids who are not being challenged to work to their potentials are still being left behind.

NOBODY'S HANDS ARE TIED

A lot of educators complain that they are bound by too many regulations. It is true that there are more legislative mandates than there used to be. As government bodies require more of schools, there gets to be less wiggle room. Still, even with the new mandates, modern educators are not without options. We cannot defy mandates, but we can work with them. If something is written into law or if it is in a contract, it should be followed. If a law or terms of a contract are bad, we should work to change them, but work within the legal guidelines. Still, mandates are not straightjackets. Educators who think that their hands are tied when given a mandate probably have not explored all of their possibilities.

Because there are so many regional, historical, socioeconomic, and individual differences among schools and students, one size will never fit all. Schools have to look at the law and decide how to best work with it. There is always a way to do things well. The mandate that everyone pass a reading test does not mean we need to emphasize reading to the exclusion of everything else. If special education students are not being challenged, IEP committees can provide more challenging curricula or placements. If the law requires that English-dominant kids who have not passed an exit test stay in an ESL program, those students can still be taught a curriculum that includes a substantial amount of material from the mainstream curriculum.

When educators get a mandate, they need to decide what's best for the kids and then work from there. It is easy to find excuses, but there is always a way to get the job done. Whenever I was told that my hands were tied, I found ways to untie them. There was wiggle room then, and there is still wiggle room now.

MY VISION FOR GARFIELD AND MY VISION FOR TWENTY-FIRST-CENTURY SCHOOLS

The vision I had at Garfield was to improve the quality of the school. I wanted to give our students a secure environment, quality instruction, and a solid curriculum. I wanted those of us in charge to take charge without thinking of consequences for ourselves. The vision bore fruit. As with mandates, models call for tinkering when there are changes in place or in time, but the Garfield model is still solid and relevant today.

Afterword

Five years ago when Gayle Gradillas, Henry Gradillas's wife, approached me about coauthoring this book, she expressed that her husband had knowledge from which educators everywhere could benefit, and that it was important that his knowledge become part of the pedagogical cannon. That certainly is the case. At that time I thought I understood the secrets of Garfield High School's success in the 1980s. I had researched, interviewed, and written about Jaime Escalante, and I had taught for most of my adult life, much of that time in schools that served low-income Hispanic students.

In the process of coauthoring this book, however, I learned that there was a lot more to Garfield High School's success than met the eye. I gained a lot of insight into both the situation at Garfield and into education in general. Dr. Gradillas's insights, attitudes, and enthusiasm have rubbed off on me. I believe that the experience of coauthoring this book has made me a better teacher, and I sincerely believe that this book will make those who read it better administrators, teachers, students, student mentors, and friends of education.

Jerry Jesness

About the Authors

Henry Gradillas was principal at Garfield High School from 1981 through 1987. He has taught science and agriculture in high schools and middle schools and has served in a number of administrative capacities. He was dean of discipline at Garfield High School, assistant principal at Belvedere Jr. High School, and principal of the Jackson Alternative School and Birmingham High School, all in the Los Angeles Unified School District. He also served as a special consultant to the California superintendent of education and as principal of Comstock High School in Kalamazoo County, Michigan. He has served as a consultant in schools throughout the United States and Canada.

He and his wife Gayle live near Ashland, Wisconsin, where he continues to work as a consultant, motivational speaker, tutor, court interpreter, and substitute teacher. He holds an EdD in curriculum from Brigham Young University, an MA in education from California State University, Los Angeles, and a BS in agronomy from the University of California, Davis.

Jerry Jesness is a teacher and writer who, in his thirty-year career, has taught English, Spanish, ESL, special education, and social studies. His writings have appeared in *Harper's*, *Reason*, *Teacher Magazine*, *Principal Magazine*, *Education Week*, *Intellectual Capital*, *Education News*, *Texas Education Review*, and several newspapers. He has published one other book, *Teaching English Language Learners K–12*.

He holds a BA in English from the University of Minnesota, Morris, and an MA in Spanish from the University of Texas, Pan American. He lives in League City, Texas, with his wife and three daughters.

Breinigsville, PA USA
20 January 2011
253754BV00001BA/2/P